Wall Highway Of Holiness

A Messianic Jewish View

by Margaret Keck

Dothan
PUBLISHING
Chagrin Falls

All scripture quotations are taken from the New King James Version.

Copyright © 2003 by Margaret Keck.

All rights reserved. No part of this publication may be reproduced, stored in a retrieval system or transmitted in any form or by any means electronic, mechanical, photocopying, recording or otherwise, without the prior written permission of the publisher except for brief quotations in books and critical reviews.

Cover: Silk painting by Linda Vinson entitled 'The Highway of Holiness'

Published by Dothan Publishing
P.O. Box 23823
Chagrin Falls OH 44023

http://www.dothanpublishing.com

International Standard Book Number (ISBN)

paper: 0-9728454-4-5

Library of Congress Control Number: 2003092848

Printed in the United States of America

Contents

INTRODUCTION	8

HOLINESS

Walking The Highway Of Holiness	10
Whom Do You Serve?	13
Understanding God	16
The Desire Of Our Hearts	19
True Humility	22

YESHUA

How Do We Spell Relief?	26
Who Is Yeshua (Jesus)?	28
Missing The Mark	32
There Is A Balm In Gilead	35

GOD'S WORD

Where To Go For Help	40
The Key To Prosperity	43
Turning Mourning Into Dancing	46
Chosen By God	49
God Fulfills His Promises	52

The Power In God's Word	54
ISRAEL	
Israel – The Chosen People	60
The God Of Second Chances	63
The Land Of Israel	66
There Is None Like You	69
SEPARATION FROM GOD	
Which Is Better Strength Or Weakness?	73
Return From The Diaspora	77
Getting Off Track	80
Finding God	83
Return And Be Healed	85
TESTNG AND TRIALS	
The Battle Is The Lord's	90
Mining For Gold	93
His Name Is Wonderful	96
Passing The Test	98
Our Deceitful Hearts	100
Restoration	102

TRAGEDIES

Turning Weakness Into Strength	107
Deadly Situations	110
My Redeemer Lives	113
When You're Having A Bad Day	115

MISTAKES

Being A Delight To God	118
Being Humble Before The Lord	120
Taking Responsibility	122
Keeping Your Focus	126

BEING WOUNDED

Should We Forgive?	130
Healing Deep Wounds	133
Preparing Against Heart Attacks	135
The Treatment of God's Anointed	139
Serving God With Joy	142

DELIVERANCE

Living In The Shadow Of Death	145
We Are Never Forsaken Or Forgotten	148
Turning Sorrow To Joy	152

Being Seen By God	**154**
Do Not Sorrow – Rejoice!	**156**
OBEDIENCE	
Doing The Right Thing	**159**
Doing Things God's Way	**163**
Following Instructions	**166**
The Importance Of Finishing	**168**
TRUSTING GOD	
Under God's Eyes	**171**
Making Up Your Mind	**175**
For This Child I Have Prayed	**177**
The Faithfulness Of God	**180**
Loss Of A Loved One	**183**
Transitions In Life	**185**
EPILOGUE	**189**

*Dedicated to my husband, Tom,
my companion on
the Highway of Holiness
and the love of my life*

Introduction

Jeremiah writes about a fire shut up in his bones. Although he tries not to speak the politically incorrect words from the Lord he is unable to be quiet. This struggle he describes as a fire shut up in his bones.

I, too, have experienced this fire. Each day for several months, the Lord quickened a scripture to me. In obedience I put my life on hold and wrote about the scripture.

At first I thought the well would never run dry. Then one day the scriptures stopped. And this prayer and devotional book was birthed.

My prayer for my readers is to walk with me on the Highway of Holiness. Experience with me God's gentle, guiding hand as He leads us with everlasting joy to Zion.

-Margaret Keck

HOLINESS

Walking The Highway Of Holiness

Isaiah 35:8-10 *⁸A highway shall be there, and a road,
And it shall be called the Highway of Holiness.
The unclean shall not pass over it,
But it shall be for others.
Whoever walks the road, although a fool,
Shall not go astray.
⁹ No lion shall be there,
Nor shall any ravenous beast go up on it;
It shall not be found there.
But the redeemed shall walk there,
¹⁰ And the ransomed of the LORD shall return,
And come to Zion with singing,
With everlasting joy on their heads.
They shall obtain joy and gladness,
And sorrow and sighing shall flee away.*

When we are traveling to a distant place, we take a map to help us find our way. God, our loving Father, is taking us on a journey bringing us to Himself. The map He provides is thousands of years old. It is His living word, the Holy Scriptures.

God has constructed a highway. This highway is not the Pacific Coast Highway or the New York Thruway. It is the Highway of Holiness.

At the tollbooth, you have to pay in order to be admitted. The price is cleanliness and purity of heart. Those who are unclean, who have defiled themselves by the filth of this world, will not be permitted to enter.

Other than that, the Highway is open to all. It is very reassuring to know even fools will not get lost. Our merits do not lead us on this Highway. Only the direction of God guides us.

Lions and ravenous beasts who try to destroy us will not be able to enter the Highway. Every wicked force on this earth will be unable to touch us. We no longer have any need to fear anything that has previously tormented us.

We will find other people on the Highway. All **the redeemed of the Lord shall walk there**. We are on the Highway not because we are bright or clever or rich or beautiful but because we have accepted Yeshua (Jesus) into our hearts. We have accepted His atoning death for our sinful state. No matter how good we might be, in God's eyes we are still sinful. Only by accepting the death of His Son do we become clean.

We, who have been bought by the price of Yeshua's (Jesus') life, can be called **the ransomed of the Lord. With singing**, we will enter Zion, the city of David where Yeshua (Jesus) will make His earthly habitation.

When we enter the city, we will be changed. We will have everlasting, unending joy and gladness. In this world, sorrow and sighing have been frequent companions. But no longer. Sorrow and sighing will vanish. We can look but they will not be there.

Do you want to walk on the Highway of Holiness?

To begin the walk there is one qualification. You have to accept the atoning death of Yeshua (Jesus) in place of your sinfulness. Sinfulness is any area of your life where you have missed the mark or the target; any place where you have failed to meet God's standards. It makes no difference if you are Jewish or gentile. Everyone needs to accept Yeshua (Jesus) in order to walk on the Highway of Holiness.

Now is the time to pray this prayer if you have never received the atoning death of Yeshua (Jesus) before or if you have wandered astray.

Dear Father,

I desire to walk on the Highway of Holiness. I want to be able to come into Your presence. I desire joy and gladness in my life. I have had my share of sorrow and sighing and I do not need anymore.

I receive the atoning death of Your Son Yeshua (Jesus) instead of my sinfulness. I desire to live a holy life, pleasing to You. I ask You to change my heart. Give me a new heart; a heart that seeks after You. Teach me Your ways.

Please forgive me for things I have done that were wrong. I do not desire to return to past bad habits and relationships. Give me the strength and guidance to go forward. I want to follow You all the days of my life and dwell with You forever.

In Yeshua's (Jesus') name I pray,

Amen

Whom Do You Serve?

2 Kings 17:33 *³³They feared the LORD, yet served their own gods—according to the rituals of the nations from among whom they were carried away.*

Assyria had dominion over Israel. The King of Assyria thought it would be a good idea to uproot the Jewish people from their land and resettle the area with his own citizens. So he relocated the inhabitants of Babylon, Cuthah, Ava Hamath and Sepharvaim into Israel. The new populace continued their worship of pagan gods.

Israel has always been set aside for the Lord. The religious practices of the new inhabitants greatly displeased the Lord; therefore, he sent lions to kill some of them. Panicked by ravenous, wild animals and in a foreign land they protested to their King. He brought a Jewish priest to educate them in the ways of God Almighty.

They had ample motivation to follow the Lord since they preferred that to being a lion's hors d'oeuvres. However, they were unwilling to leave behind their pagan gods and worship wholeheartedly the God of Abraham, Isaac and Jacob.

The choice given to these pagan refugees is the same choice God gives to all of us. Are we willing to lay aside all vestiges and attachments to pagan practices and worship God alone?

We try to justify our behavior by the things we do. We may attend services once or twice a week and be active in various outreaches of our congregation. Is this all God is asking of us?

God is not only interested in what we do but rather in who we are.

Do we follow Him with all our heart, soul and strength?

Do we prefer Him to Monday Night Football or Oprah?

Do we guard our mouths so that no gossip falls from our lips?

In the morning, after we read the Holy Scriptures do we read our horoscope in the newspaper?

After we finish praying on the prayer chain, do we watch soap operas or pick up a new romance novel at the grocery?

Are we totally committed to the Lord regardless of the price?

Will we risk being ostracized by family and friends in order to follow Him?

Have these questions introduced other questionable areas in your life? Do you desire to get rid of your growling lions? Do you desire a purer walk with God, free from unholy influences?

If so then pray the following prayer.

Dear Father,

Forgive me for being double minded. It seems to others that I follow You but You know my heart has strayed into other areas. Forgive me for _____ (list the things you do that are not pleasing to the Lord.) I ask You to give me the strength to overcome these things.

I desire your holiness in my life. I desire when people see me they see You. I want to be Your hands, feet and heart on this earth. I desire to touch others who do not know You. I desire to reach others with the Gospel. I desire to care for others the way You care for me.

Free me Lord from every unholy influence binding me from worshiping You. I know, only through You, do I have real freedom. I choose freedom and not slavery. Strengthen me in areas where I am weak. Help me to lose interest in things not good for me. Renew my life.

Thank You for being my God who always hears me when I cry. Thank You for changing my life.

In Yeshua's (Jesus') name,

Amen

Understanding God

Jeremiah 9:23-24 *²³Thus says the LORD:*
"Let not the wise man glory in his wisdom,
Let not the mighty man glory in his might,
Nor let the rich man glory in his riches;
²⁴ But let him who glories glory in this,
That he understands and knows Me,
That I am the LORD, exercising lovingkindness, judgment,
 and righteousness in the earth.
For in these I delight," says the LORD.

Understanding God takes a lifetime. When we first become believers, our conception of God may be influenced by our relationship with our earthly father. As we grow and mature, our understanding of the scriptures shapes our image of God. The longer we walk with the Lord the more we see Him manifested in our lives. Therefore, our day-to-day experience also forms our idea of God's identity.

The more we know about God we realize how little we actually know Him. With our finite minds, we try to grasp the infinite and always fall short. We realize the better we know Him the more there is to know.

A good starting place is to examine some of the qualities God possesses.

Lovingkindness is inexorably linked to mercy. When God's lovingkindness, mercy, compassion, forgiveness, sympathy, empathy and understanding manifest in our lives we are changed. We are unaccustomed to unconditional outpourings of lovingkindness in our lives. However, once we experience it we can then be vessels of lovingkindness to others.

Judgment involves a verdict be it favorable or unfavorable, a determination, an order, or a sentence. Regardless of whether or not it fits our theological doctrine, the fact is God is a God of judgment. God judges us upon our actions. Judgment is not always adverse. We have to recognize we are responsible for our actions and ultimately we are judged.

Righteousness is making right. We do not have any righteousness compared to God. Our righteousness pales before His. Only by walking in His righteousness can we succeed.

Nevertheless, at times we are all guilty in glorying or boasting in our own talents and abilities. The college professor will boast in his knowledge. The Olympic weight lifter will glory in his strength. The millionaire will glory in his money.

God has given us all certain talents and abilities but they are feeble in contrast to God's traits. Instead of acknowledging our insignificance, we often choose to ignore God's presence in our lives.

We are stuck on ourselves. It is very difficult to get unstuck. If we truly want to begin to understand God, we need to:

- ❖ Turn our inward focus outward toward the Lord
- ❖ Stop patting ourselves on the back and start thanking God for our gifting
- ❖ Pray for teachable spirits to be able to learn about God
- ❖ Desire for God to delight in us

The first step in understanding God is through prayer.

Dear Holy God,

Even though I call myself a believer there is so much I do not understand about You. I ask You to give me understanding about Yourself. I very much want to be a delight to You. I ask You to open my eyes to Your lovingkindness, judgment and righteousness in my life. Teach me how to understand You.

Help me to get my eyes off myself. Fill my heart with Your presence.

In Yeshua's (Jesus') name I pray,

Amen

The Desire Of Our Hearts

Solomon's Petition

I Kings 3:7-9 *⁷Now, O LORD my God, You have made Your servant king instead of my father David, but I am a little child; I do not know how to go out or come in. ⁸And Your servant is in the midst of Your people whom You have chosen, a great people, too numerous to be numbered or counted. ⁹Therefore give to Your servant an understanding heart to judge Your people, that I may discern between good and evil.*

God's Answer

I Kings 3:12-13 *¹²behold, I have done according to your words; see, I have given you a wise and understanding heart, so that there has not been anyone like you before you, nor shall any like you arise after you. ¹³And I have also given you what you have not asked: both riches and honor, so that there shall not be anyone like you among the kings all your days.*

After opposition from his brother, Adonijah, Solomon assumes the throne of Israel and Judah. In a dream, God comes to him and asks him what he wants. God has laid the potential for Solomon's ownership of the entire world within his grasp. Solomon's response pleases God.

- ❖ Solomon acknowledges it was God; **You have made Your servant king**, who chose him above his brother to assume leadership of the country. Solomon realizes God, influencing men, designates all appointments of headship over countries.
- ❖ Even though Solomon is ruler of Israel he says, **"but I am a little child."** Few men or women in powerful positions would describe themselves as little children. Be-

ing childlike suggests a humble spirit and a person willing to learn.

❖ In fact, Solomon further states that **he does not know how to go out or come in**. He was not referring to the operation of a door. He was applying an idiom meaning he was open to teaching.

❖ Solomon grasps the enormity of his new position. **And Your servant is in the midst of Your people whom You have chosen, a great people, too numerous to be numbered or counted.** Yet this awareness does not make him arrogant or over confident.

❖ Out of the abundance of the world, Solomon asks for one thing. **Therefore give to Your servant an understanding heart to judge Your people.** In Hebrew the word for understanding is שָׁמַע (sham ah) and it literally means hearing, in the sense of being obedient. Very often people say one thing but mean another. It often takes discernment to discover a person's true motive.

❖ Solomon desires this quality to be exalted but to be a good and just ruler able to **discern between good and evil.**

God's answer to Solomon's petition goes beyond what he asked. God will do the same for us when the desires of our hearts are pleasing to Him.

What is the desire of your heart? Now is your time to approach the throne of grace.

Dear Father,

I come to You in Yeshua's (Jesus') name. I desire, as Solomon did, to have an understanding heart able to discern between good and evil. I humble myself before You and come as a little child, asking You to teach me. I do not desire great wealth or power but only to be of service in Your kingdom. Please teach me the things I need to know. Increase my discernment between good and evil. Enable me to love good and hate evil.

Thank You for being my God who hears my prayers.

Amen

True Humility

Isaiah 6:5 *⁵"Woe is me, for I am undone!*
Because I am a man of unclean lips,
And I dwell in the midst of a people of unclean lips;
For my eyes have seen the King,
The LORD of hosts."

Isaiah was a man of true humility. He walked wearing the mantle of a prophet. He appeared unafraid before kings and princes. He spoke forth unpopular sentiments. He criticized the behavior of rulers. He clearly proclaimed the message of the Lord.

Never once, was he described as being humble and yet there is not a clearer example of true humility than his exclamation, **"Woe is me, for I am undone!"** There is a deep groaning in his spirit as he proclaims his humbleness.

He has seen the Lord of Hosts. God is the commander-in-chief of thousands upon thousands of warriors. Being in God's presence focuses Isaiah's attention on his own situation.

Isaiah was not an evil person with hidden sin in his life. At an early age he was chosen by God to declare His messages to His people. He faithfully performed all that was required of him.

Yet in the presence of the Lord, he is overcome with his own shortcomings. He says he is undone דָּמָה (da ma) which has a stronger meaning in the Hebrew. It also means to be silent or to be destroyed.

When you are destroyed, there is not a lot left. All his earthly accomplishments have vanished. In the presence of God, there is only true humbleness. In fact, he takes this a step further asserting that he is **"a man of unclean lips."**

This is the same man who spoke forth God's judgment and yet he says he has unclean lips. The fuller meaning of unclean is foul in a religious sense, defiled, infamous, and polluted.

Everyone Isaiah knows also has unclean lips. We can all fit in that category as well. We become truly humble in the presence of God.

There is a mistaken conception concerning humility. Very often we believe if we speak poorly of ourselves in front of others then this is being humble. Or if we live simply and deny ourselves then this is humility. This is all worldly humility.

Godly humility is seeing ourselves, as Isaiah did, in the presence of the Lord. Our righteousness is as filthy rags. Our lips are unclean in comparison to the purity of the Lord.

In order to manifest Godly humility we need to seek God's presence.

Dear Holy Father,

I come seeking Your presence in my life. I do not want to walk in worldly humility. I want Godly humility. I ask You to reveal Yourself to me in a deeper way than I have ever before experienced.

I desire to be a pleasing vessel of use for You. Use me for Your glory not my own. Deliver me from worldly conceptions of humility. Move in power in my life.

In Yeshua's (Jesus') name I pray,

Amen

JESHUA

How Do We Spell Relief?
YESHUA

Isaiah 45:22-25 [22] *"Look to Me, and be saved,*
All you ends of the earth!
For I am God, and there is no other.
[23] *I have sworn by Myself;*
The word has gone out of My mouth in righteousness,
And shall not return,
That to Me every knee shall bow,
Every tongue shall take an oath.
[24] *He shall say,*
'Surely in the LORD I have righteousness and strength.
To Him men shall come,
And all shall be ashamed
Who are incensed against Him.
[25] *In the LORD all the descendants of Israel*
Shall be justified, and shall glory.'"

People are constantly searching for ways to gain relief. We try Eastern meditation, yoga, Scientology, channelers, fortune-tellers, gematria, palmistry, astrology, magic 8 balls, and Ouija boards; anything and everything that promises answers to our problems.

But God says, **"Look to Me, and be saved."** The word saved in Hebrew is יָשַׁע (ya sha) and means to be free, safe, defended, delivered, helped, preserved, rescued, to bring salvation, and to get victory. The root word יָשַׁע is the same root for the name of Yeshua (Jesus) which means He is our salvation, freer, defender, deliverer, helper, preserver, rescuer and victory.

We do not have to look in obscure corners for answers. How could it be plainer? God says we are to look to Him. Is it just some people who are to look to Him? No. Everyone, everywhere, even to the **ends of the earth** is to look to Him.

There is no other God, no other remedy, no other religion, and no other way. God does not give us a great deal of latitude. God has taken an oath proclaiming He is ruler of all. Every person and spirit must profess allegiance to Him.

Our enemies are not only physical they are also spiritual. Spirits of depression, oppression, anger, rebellion, grief, sadness, shame, doubt, fear, etc. cannot control our lives because in **the LORD all the descendants of Israel shall be justified, and shall glory.**

We must appropriate this promise of victory whether we are tormented by people or spiritual forces. By praying this scripture, God guarantees us that our enemies will not triumph over us.

Our belief influences our behavior. If we think we are defeated, we will act as if we are defeated. The reality is that we are victorious. We are to look to God as our defender. He will not fail us.

Dear Father,

I look to You for relief in my life. You know the circumstances bearing down heavily upon me. I refuse to continue believing the lies of my physical and spiritual enemies. I am not a victim but a victor through Yeshua (Jesus) the Messiah.

I come against every stronghold keeping me captive. I break every generational curse upon me and my family from five gen-

erations back on each side of my family. I am free, delivered, rescued and victorious in Messiah Yeshua (Jesus).

I believe there is only one God with three manifestations as the Father, Yeshua (Jesus) the Son, and the Ruach (Holy Spirit). I will no longer follow the teaching of any other that denies the sovereignty of God. I will remove all books, tapes, CD's, videos, etc. from my house that exalt any man over my Lord God.

I ask You to show me if there is anything displeasing to You in my house, car or office. I desire to walk the Highway of Holiness.

Thank You for hearing and answering my prayer.

In Yeshua's (Jesus') name I pray,

Amen

Who Is Yeshua (Jesus)?

Isaiah 42:1-4 *¹"Behold! My Servant whom I uphold, My Elect One in whom My soul delights! I have put My Spirit upon Him; He will bring forth justice to the gentiles. ² He will not cry out, nor raise His voice, Nor cause His voice to be heard in the street. ³ A bruised reed He will not break, And smoking flax He will not quench; He will bring forth justice for truth. ⁴ He will not fail nor be discouraged, Till He has established justice in the earth; And the coastlands shall wait for His law."*

There are several ways we get to know a person:
- ❖ By speaking to him
- ❖ By listening to him
- ❖ By looking at what he has done
- ❖ By learning about him from others

Yeshua (Jesus) is a person, who took on humanity, as well as being God. We can become better acquainted with Yeshua using the same methods we do with friends.

We *speak* to Yeshua (Jesus) through prayer. We are instructed in the Holy Scriptures to pray to God our Father in the name of Yeshua. He is the intermediary or the bridge between the Father and us. All relationships become very one sided and boring if we do all the talking.

There is a time for *listening*. Listening to Yeshua (Jesus) is often through the Ruach Ha Kodesh (the Holy Spirit). Impressions, thoughts and feelings can often be methods of communication from the Ruach (Spirit.)

We can *judge the work* of Yeshua (Jesus) by the changed lives in our self and in others.

We can know Yeshua (Jesus) better is by *learning about Him from others*. The prophet Isaiah paints a vivid portrait of our Messiah.

1) The Father has chosen Him and delights in Him. **He has God's Spirit** רוּחַ (ruach) on Him. God's Spirit is translated as His very breath. We know His Ruach is His Holy Spirit.

2) One of Yeshua's jobs is to bring **justice to the gentiles**. Justice מִשְׁפָּט (mish pat) is also translated as judgment.

3) The concept that Yeshua (Jesus) is the God of the gentiles is not entirely correct. God, the father, selected the Jewish people as His chosen ones from all the nations. In fact, the meaning of gentile גּוֹי (goy) is any people or nation other than Israel or the Jewish people. Therefore, God will not only judge the Jews, which was common knowledge in the days of Isaiah but the gentiles as well.

4) Yeshua was not an attention-seeker; **He will not cry out, raise His voice or cause His voice to be heard in the streets.** On the contrary, He will be modest, calm and settled.

5) He is described as **a bruised reed**. Bruised in the Hebrew is רָצַץ (ra tsa) and means break, bruise, crush, discourage, oppress, and struggle together. From all we know some leaders attempted to break, bruise, crush, discourage, oppress, struggle against and ultimately kill Yeshua. Nevertheless, they did not succeed. He did not break, was not crushed, was not discouraged, was not oppressed, and is not dead.

6) He was described as **a smoking flax** or a wick of a candle that has been blown out. But, surprise, He will not be extinguished. It might look as though the enemy has triumphed but he has not. The flame of the candle, which was almost extinguished relights and burns brightly.

7) Often we hear complaints that things are not fair. The only justice we are promised is by the acts of Yeshua. He will bring **justice into all the earth**.

Getting to know Yeshua takes a lifetime.

Dear Father,

I come to You wanting more. I want to know Yeshua better, I want to know You better, I want to know Your Spirit better. I desire a deeper relationship with You. Teach me things I have not known before. Lead me places I have not gone before. Reveal things to me I have not seen before. Open Your word to me and train me to be the person You desire me to be.

In the past, if I have accepted some things as true that are not then I ask You to reeducate me. I desire Your truth not man's lies.

Just as You called Abraham Your friend, I desire the same. I want to know You better.

Amen

Missing The Mark

Isaiah 1:18 *¹⁸"Come now, and let us reason together,"*
Says the LORD,
"Though your sins are like scarlet,
They shall be as white as snow;
Though they are red like crimson,
They shall be as wool.

Are you a good person?

Do you ever sin?

It may be surprising to some, but good people do sin. Confusion enters because we do not understand the Hebrew definition of the word sin. One meaning of sin is to miss the mark. Picture an archery target. You pull the arrow back in the bow. The arrow flies but misses the target let alone the bull's eye. You have missed the mark.

Now picture a situation where you and God have targeted goals, be it raising your children, relationships with your spouse, parents, siblings or neighbors. Are there times when you fall short of your or God's desired aim?

Would you call this sin?

God would. Sin is not just stealing, killing and harming others. Even if we have allowed Yeshua (Jesus) to enter our hearts and be our Lord we still sin. There is not one person who never sins. We all do.

Sin is sin regardless of the degree. However, the consequences of sin vary. For example, you will not be put in prison for jaywalking but would be for murder.

This scripture compares sin to the scarlet dye. The dye, gathered from a worm or insect, was so strong that it was impossible to be removed. That is what our sins, big or small, are like.

We cannot do anything to get rid of them. No amount of good deeds will wipe away our sins. No amount of 'I'm sorry" will wipe away our sins. No amount of self-condemnation or regret will wipe away our sins.

Only God can and will wipe away our sins. In fact, He does not merely wipe them away He transforms this indelible crimson dye into being as **white as snow.** There is nothing cleaner or purer than freshly fallen white snow.

You can have this purity in your life and in your heart. Ask God to forgive you for things you have done to miss the mark. Now is the time to invite God into your heart. Accept His love for you. Accept the death of Yeshua (Jesus) on the tree. Yeshua (Jesus) took your place. Once Yeshua (Jesus) lives in your heart, you are assured of eternal life. Your physical body will fade away but your spiritual body will live forever with Yeshua (Jesus).

If you want to be clean then pray this prayer.

Dear Father,

I come to You overwhelmed with my sin. I never considered myself a bad person but I have done things that are not right. I know in Your eyes they are sin. I know that no matter how large or small my sins are You still forgive me.

I ask for Your forgiveness. I do not want to continue behaving this way. I ask You to set me free and cleanse me from all unrighteousness. Guide and lead me in all I do. Move in great power in my life.

I believe that Yeshua (Jesus) is Your Son. I ask Him to come into my heart and atone for my sins by His blood. I believe He died for my sins so that I can have eternal life.

I thank You for being a great God, being able to transform me.

In Yeshua's (Jesus') precious name I pray,

Amen

There Is A Balm In Gilead

Jeremiah 8:21-22 *²¹For the hurt of the daughter of my people I am hurt.*
I am mourning;
Astonishment has taken hold of me.
²² Is there no balm in Gilead,
Is there no physician there?
Why then is there no recovery
For the health of the daughter of my people?

Jeremiah, the weeping prophet, travails in prayer for his people. Jeremiah, like Shaul (Paul) in the Brit Hadasha (New Covenant) empathizes so closely with the plight of his people that he experiences the pain from her brokenness.

The word **hurt** describing the condition of the representative daughter, is שֶׁבֶר (she ver) and means an affliction, breach, breaking, broken, bruise, destruction, hurt, or vexation. It is not a superficial wound. It is a deep brokenness. Jeremiah goes into mourning as if she had already died.

Another meaning for **astonishment** is desolation. Desolation has taken hold of Jeremiah. Desolation implies the total lack of hope. It is as if all is lost.

Jeremiah cries out for the healing ointment or **balm in Gilead.** Is there no one to treat this unbearable grief? Where is the doctor? Does this mean that the daughter will never recover?

How many of us have asked God, with tear-stained faces, to heal our wounds be they physical, spiritual or emotional? How many of us have wondered where our healer is? How many of us have been in despair?

We can rejoice because there is a balm in Gilead. His name is Yeshua (Jesus). No matter your pain, trial or desperate circumstances there is a healer who can soothe your every ache.

God heard Jeremiah's cry and answered. However, if we never apply Yeshua's (Jesus') healing touch to our lives it is as if there is no remedy. Yeshua is waiting for us to reach out our bleeding hands and hearts to receive His soothing balm.

The world can say our situation is hopeless. Yeshua (Jesus) specializes in hopeless cases. We place our faith in the medical profession; we place our faith in lawyers; we place our faith in men. However, do we place our faith in God? Do we expect God to heal us when it hurts?

It seems our 'expecter' runs on budget batteries and often fails after a little while. We can expectantly look for relief for a few hours. We can even sustain our faith for a few days. How about for a few months or for a few years?

The only way to recharge our faith batteries is through immersing ourselves in God's word and God's promises. His promises have to become more real than the doctor's bad report or the terrible situation confronting us daily.

There is a balm in Gilead who will heal you every place it hurts. Reach out to receive God's healing touch for your life. Open your hands to accept all God has for you. God is trustworthy. Trust Him.

Dear Father,

Only You know the full extent of the horrible situation in my life. I urgently need Your healing balm of Gilead in my heart, body, mind and spirit. I hurt so badly. I cannot even stand to think about my situation.

I open my hands wide to receive Your healing. I take Your balm of Gilead, Yeshua HaMashiach, (Jesus, the Messiah) and apply it to all my torn and bleeding places. I believe You can make me whole again. I believe You can take horrifying situations and turn them around for Your glory.

I believe You will do these things only because You love me. Even though at times I am very unlovable, You still love me. I do not have to put on a religious face for You to take care of me. You allowed Your only begotten Son to die on a tree for me. I accept His death for my redemption. He not only died for my sins but also for my sicknesses. I believe that.

Thank You for loving me so much.

In Yeshua's (Jesus') name I pray,

Amen

GOD'S WORD

Where To Go For Help

Isaiah 31:1-3 *[1] Woe to those who go down to Egypt for help,
And rely on horses,
Who trust in chariots because they are many,
And in horsemen because they are very strong,
But who do not look to the Holy One of Israel,
Nor seek the LORD!
[2] Yet He also is wise and will bring disaster,
And will not call back His words,
But will arise against the house of evildoers,
And against the help of those who work iniquity.
[3] Now the Egyptians are men, and not God;
And their horses are flesh, and not spirit.
When the LORD stretches out His hand,
Both he who helps will fall,
And he who is helped will fall down;
They all will perish together.*

In the face of a serious dilemma, to whom do you look for help?

Do you immediately pick up the phone and dial your friend, your lawyer, your doctor, your stockbroker?

Do you rush to the medicine cabinet and take some tranquilizers?

Do you become overwhelmed and go to bed even in the middle of the day?

There are many valid ways of dealing with troubles but there is only one right way. Clearly, we are advised not to **go down to**

Egypt for help. Egypt stands for the power and strength of men.

Egypt has horses and chariots. Their weapons of warfare are physical. Moreover, they triumph in the physical arena. However, are our problems exclusively in the physical realm? No. There, most assuredly, are physical or natural ramifications but there are also, equally significant, spiritual implications.

We tend to overlook the spiritual implications and attempt to deal solely with the physical element. We treat the symptom but not the underlying cause. We may briefly gain relief but because the root cause is untreated, the symptom can change its form and return.

God very clearly tells us to seek Him when disaster falls. God does not leave us defenseless. The Holy Scriptures are full of promises for our well-being. It is our option to choose or refuse these promises. Reading them alone does a small amount of good. However, it is necessary for them to become part of our body of knowledge, to inscribe them in our heart and in our mind. They need to become as real to us as eating and drinking.

Keep a journal. Record God's promises and repeat them back to Him personalized with you and your family's names. Read them aloud so you not only see it with your eyes but also hear it with your ears.

God tells us He will not change His promises, **and will not call back His words.** If He has promised you things, He will keep His word. In addition, He will fight for you in the physical, spiritual, and emotional realm. **He will arise against the house of evildoers, And against the help of those who work iniquity.**

Sometimes it is necessary to persevere. Jacob wrestled with God until daybreak. He would not let go. We need to persist and not give up.

God warns us against relying on the material things of this world for help. His forecast is failure for us and those who help us. **Now the Egyptians are men, and not God; And their horses are flesh, and not spirit. When the LORD stretches out His hand, Both he who helps will fall, And he who is helped will fall down; They all will perish together.**

On the other hand, God is not saying do not take medications or consult specialists. He is saying He must come first. He can use things of this world to help us. We need to be sure our hearts are right with God. We need to be sure He is number one. We need to be sure we do not doubt His strength. We need to be sure we are in a right relationship with Him. We need to be sure we spend more time with Him then we do in the doctor's waiting room.

If you need God's help appropriate His promises. Ingrain His words in your heart and in your mind. Seek His face in all situations.

Dear Father,

I ask You and Your word to be more real to me then they have ever been before. I desire to put You first at all times in my life. I desire Your strength. I will not look to the world as my only hope. You are my hope. I commit my life to You.

In Yeshua's (Jesus') name I pray,

Amen

The Key To Prosperity

Psalm 1:1-3 *¹Blessed is the man
Who walks not in the counsel of the ungodly,
Nor stands in the path of sinners,
Nor sits in the seat of the scornful;
² But his delight is in the law of the LORD,
And in His law he meditates day and night.
³ He shall be like a tree
Planted by the rivers of water,
That brings forth its fruit in its season,
Whose leaf also shall not wither;
And whatever he does shall prosper.*

We all seek prosperity, be it financial, emotional, physical or spiritual. Prosperity, in this psalm, means more than financial security. The Hebrew root of the word prosper is צָלֵחַ (tza ley ah), and means to push forward, break out, come (mightily), be good, be profitable, and/or to prosper.

We all have areas in our lives where we need to push forward. Sometimes we feel as if we are stuck. We can be stuck in our jobs, stuck in relationships or stuck in problems. Biblical prosperity has the power to push us forward and to break us out of the area trapping us.

King David establishes guidelines to follow in order to insure prosperity.
   1) **We are not**
         a. to seek or follow advice from **ungodly counselors.**
         b. to be on the same track as **sinners** (those who miss the mark.)

   c. to be like **the scornful,** mockers, or those who ridicule.
 2) **We are to**
   a. **delight** or derive pleasure **in the law** תּוֹרָה (Torah)
   b. **think about God's word both day and night**

We live in a fallen world where the wicked seem to prosper. If we are caught off guard, we may try to emulate the ways of the world. We look to quick fixes to long standing problems. The glitziness of passing fads draws us in. We are tempted to follow anything or anyone who is successful in the world's eyes.

If we seek God's prosperity, we need to dwell in His word. We need to enjoy reading the Bible as much or more than hot fudge sundaes (you can fill in your favorite dessert.) We need to smack our lips over every bite. We need to set our minds on the things we have learned and digested from God's word. This knowledge should sit at the forefront of our minds.

If we follow these rules then God promises us certain things.
 1) We will be like **trees planted near rivers of water**
   a. we will never be hungry
   b. we will be able to eat whenever we want
   c. we will never have to worry about food
 2) **We will bring forth fruit at the appropriate time**
   a. we will not be barren
   b. we will be productive
   c. our timing for producing will be perfect
 3) **Our leaves will not wither**
   a. we will not have seasons of dryness
   b. we will not be left alone (without any leaves)
 4) **Whatever we do will prosper**

It is important to pray God's promises into the essence of our beings. So we will not be shaken by the storms of this world.

Dear Father,

I come to You in Yeshua's name. I desire Your prosperity in my life and in the lives of my family. I ask You to increase my desire to read and absorb Your word. Help me to delight in Your scriptures and in You.

Turn my heart away from the world and worldly values. I desire Godly values in my life.

I ask You to help me break any relationships in my life that are ungodly and unhealthy. Help me to leave situations not pleasing to You.

I desire Your prosperity in my life.

I give You permission to change my life.

In the name of Your son, I pray,

Amen

Turning Mourning Into Dancing

Jeremiah 32:27 [27] *"Behold, I am the LORD, the God of all flesh. Is there anything too hard for Me?*

In this life, we all face difficult situations that wound our hearts. The situations generally involve other people. Those we love the most wound us the most deeply. This category usually includes our spouse, children and parents.

We carry our bleeding hearts in our hands as we search for help. We go to psychologists, psychiatrists, friends, rabbis, pastors and doctors. We read magazines, books and newspapers looking for a cure for our broken hearts. We surf the internet and e-mail friends far and wide looking for a panacea for our problem.

Unfortunately, all our self-help fixes generally fall short. They may be a temporary solution but the deep-seated pain in our hearts remains. That was the bad news. The good news is the existence of a permanent solution that eliminates the pain. Our situation may not change immediately but our grieving will be replaced by rejoicing.

The key factor in this transformation is our belief in God. There is no room for, "I believe but…" God is either who He says He is and will perform what He promises or He is not. There are times when our faith wavers. God knows this will happen. That is a reason He gave us His word, the Holy Scriptures.

Using a lexicon gives greater depth to the scriptures by allowing us to understand the meanings of the original Greek and Hebrew words. Merely reading the Bible is insufficient. Merely listening to sermons is insufficient. God will quicken words in scripture upon closer examination.

God's word is like no other. It has supernatural power to heal a broken heart. However, if you never open it, it can never accomplish what God intentioned for it.

Right now, we can use the promise in Jeremiah to heal every wound in every heart. First God says, **"I am the Lord."** The Hebrew word is יְהֹוָה (y' ho vah) and means eternal. God is not here today and gone tomorrow. He has been here since before the formation of the earth and He does not plan on leaving. We can trust Someone who will always be there.

Next, He tells us His job description. He is **the God of all flesh.** There is no person we know without flesh. Therefore, our God is his God. It does not matter if he does not acknowledge God. That does not change the fact.

In conclusion, God says, **"Is their anything too hard for me?"** That is a rhetorical question. The answer is no, nada, nothing! The situation grieving your heart is not too hard for God.

The Hebrew word for hard is פָּלָא (pa la) and has a range of meanings, great, difficult, wonderful, hard, hidden, things too high, marvelous, miraculous, and wondrous. God can do it all.

However, on occasion the process takes some time. Our answer does not always come as soon as the prayer leaves our lips. During this waiting period, Satan gets busy in our hearts. He looses doubt, fear and unbelief. This unholy threesome whisper nagging fears and half-truths into our hearts.

Whenever there is a setback in our situation, the threesome work overtime trying to have us forget God's word, power and promise. We dwell on the bad news. The threesome whisper future compounding problems into our ears and as a result, we despair. We stop praying because we believe there is no hope.

These are all lies. We must cling to the word of God and never let go.

Dear Father,

I come to You in Yeshua's (Jesus') name. A situation burdens my heart. I lift it up to You now. (Pause and speak it to the Lord). Every time I think of this situation and the one I love, I will remember Your promise.

I will not let the enemy drag me into his pit. Even though I do not have the answer to my problem, I believe You are aware and active in it. I will not carry it as a burden. I release it to You.

I believe You can do wondrous, marvelous, and miraculous things in this situation.

Thank You for being a God I can believe in and trust. Thank You for Your word that brings life.

In Your Son's name I pray,

Amen

Chosen By God

Isaiah 44:1-5 *¹ "Yet hear me now, O Jacob My servant,*
And Israel whom I have chosen.
² Thus says the LORD who made you
And formed you from the womb, who will help you:
'Fear not, O Jacob My servant;
And you, Jeshurun, whom I have chosen.
³ For I will pour water on him who is thirsty,
And floods on the dry ground;
I will pour My Spirit on your descendants,
And My blessing on your offspring;
⁴ They will spring up among the grass
Like willows by the watercourses.'
⁵ One will say, 'I am the LORD'S';
Another will call himself by the name of Jacob;
Another will write with his hand, 'The LORD'S,'
And name himself by the name of Israel.

God is speaking to Israel and to those who align themselves with Israel and are believers in Messiah Yeshua (Jesus).

We think we choose God but actually, it is God who has **chosen** us. Not only did He choose us but He also **formed** or squeezed us into shape. He created us from a single cell into complex beings.

For added emphasis, God says twice that He has chosen us. This is something we need to imprint in our minds and hearts. God has **chosen** us. Out of many, he picked us.

This is not a cause for fear. Since God has **chosen** us, Satan has also chosen us as an enemy and a target. Satan hates those who God loves. However, when the attacks come God is telling us in advance not to be afraid.

Jeshurun is another name for Israel first used by Moses in Deuteronomy 32:15. There is no denying that the state of Israel is still God's chosen; Satan is not happy as evidenced by all the blood being shed in that tiny country.

Why are we chosen?

We are chosen because we are **thirsty** for the presence of God in our lives. God knows our thirst and promises to **pour living water** upon us. When we are filled with living water, our thirst is quenched. Yeshua (Jesus) is the living water.

Areas in our life that are dry, parched ground will be renewed by the flood of God's living water. We have a wonderful promise that God will **pour His Spirit on our descendants,** not only our children and grandchildren and perhaps even great-grandchildren but on all our descendants ad infinitum.

There is also a blessing on all of our children.

- ❖ They will be numerous
- ❖ They will not be lacking just as the willows are richly fed by the water
- ❖ They will identify themselves as believers

The blessing on our children contains three different aspects. One will say he is **the LORD'S** meaning he identifies with being a member of God's family. Just as we say we are a Smith, Jones, Cohen, or Goldman so our children will say that they are of God's family. **Another will call himself** or identify himself as being part of Israel or **Jacob.** And the third **will write** either **with his hand** or on his hand **that he is of Israel.**

God is speaking His blessing over our children first in general, then more specifically and finally individually. This is a wonderful blessing for us to speak over our own children.

Dear Father,

I lift up not only my children but also my family and all my descendants. I appropriate Your blessings for them. I receive Your living water on all the dry and thirsty places in my life. I thank You for Your renewal in the desert areas I am walking through.

I thank You for loving me so much that You care about everything that I care about. In particular, You share in my concern for my children. I receive Your blessings upon my children. I do not look with physical eyes but with my spiritual eyes. I see all my children and descendants loving You with all their heart, mind and soul.

Thank You for loving me.

In Yeshua's (Jesus') name I pray,

Amen

God Fulfills His Promises

Isaiah 55:10-11 *[10]"For as the rain comes down, and the snow from heaven,*
And do not return there,
But water the earth,
And make it bring forth and bud,
That it may give seed to the sower
And bread to the eater,
[11] *So shall My word be that goes forth from My mouth;*
It shall not return to Me void,
But it shall accomplish what I please,
And it shall prosper in the thing for which I sent it.

Reading the Holy Scriptures with our eyes alone will not reap the full benefits of God's promises. Our eyes bring the words into our mind. However, the mind is very cluttered, full of thoughts about issues at work, the shopping list for the grocery store, the current political situation ad infinitum. God's word becomes another fleeting thought, here for a minute and then gone.

If we wish for life changing, miraculous answers to problems then we need to incorporate God's word into our body of knowledge. We all have a belief system that governs our responses to various situations. Our belief system is a product of our parents' instruction, life experience, and our self-determination.

To integrate God's word into our body of knowledge is difficult because it often contradicts the rules of this world. For example, it is not common to teach that those who serve will be exalted. But our Messiah came as a suffering servant and is now seated at the right hand of God. It is His behavior we are to emulate.

God gives us the Holy Scriptures to teach, guide, deliver, encourage and renew us. It is our job to digest it. There are several ways to accomplish this:

- ❖ Do your daily reading aloud. In that way, your ears hear the words your eyes are seeing. Then you are absorbing with two different senses.
- ❖ When the Lord quickens a verse to you, write it down in a notebook. Periodically review your verses.
- ❖ Choose certain verses to keep before your eyes, on the refrigerator, mirror, or dashboard.
- ❖ Personalize your chosen verses.
- ❖ When praying speak the verses, reminding God of His promises to you and your family.
- ❖ Keep your focus on God and His promises and not on your problems.

God's word is similar to the rain and snow. It has a purpose to fulfill. The rain and snow water the earth providing nourishment for plants. These plants are harvested and produce a crop. We take the harvest and make it into food, which then nourishes our bodies.

Likewise, God's word becomes food for us. God speaks His word directing it to accomplish specific purposes in our lives. His word will not return to Him empty. It will successfully fulfill God's purpose.

God wants you to be successful. Your concerns are His concerns. Let Him help you reach your goals. Appropriate His promises into the essence of your being. Never let them go.

Dear Father,

I want Your promises for prosperity and success in my life. Help me to remember Your promises. Keep my eyes focused on You and not on myself or my situation.

Thank You for caring so much for me that You provide a way for me to rise above my circumstances. I receive all You have for me.

In Yeshua's (Jesus') name I pray,

Amen

The Power In God's Word

Jeremiah 23:29 *²⁹"Is not My word like a fire?" says the LORD,*
"And like a hammer that breaks the rock in pieces?

If we truly understood the power in God's word, our entire orientation would change. The Orthodox Jews revere the word of God so highly that when any Bible or prayer book touches the ground they kiss it. How many of us have seen preachers, when trying to make a point, literally stand on top of a Bible? Or how many of us place our Bibles on the floor for safekeeping?

Would we treat dynamite the way we treat the word of God? We have an explosive far more powerful than any bomb known on earth. It functions in two ways: as a consuming fire devouring everything in its path and as a pounding hammer shattering all opposition.

God says it very plainly. His **word is like a fire and like a hammer that breaks the rock in pieces**. Applying and appropriating God's word into our lives and into difficult situations will transform things. If the fuse is never placed in a stick of dynamite, there is no way to direct it. If we do not apply God's promises to areas of darkness, how can we expect results?

The context of this verse concerns false prophets who lie to people. Today we also have false prophets. We have gurus masquerading as messengers from God spreading worship of false gods. Many of our family and friends have been lured into these false teachings. Satan has blinded their eyes to the truth of God.

Only the word of God will deliver them. The word can be applied in various ways.

- ❖ By bringing scriptures to their attention refuting their teaching
- ❖ By praying for them using targeted scriptures
- ❖ By personalizing scriptures with their names
- ❖ By acting in a scriptural way toward them (speaking the truth in love)
- ❖ By not falling into Satan's trap of discouragement and despair but always expecting God's deliverance in their lives

It is not wise or necessary to become an expert on every foul, false teaching in the world. The internet is a valuable resource for discovering responses to false religions. Go to a search engine and type in 'Christianity versus whatever' and very often articles will appear from trusted sources refuting the counterfeit religion.

Your prayers will make a difference. Claiming scriptures for them will focus your prayers. Placing their names in the scriptures will further narrow the focus until your prayer becomes a laser beam, burning deeply.

Quoting scripture and praying for your loved ones may fall short if you are not behaving in a scriptural way toward them. Actions may not speak louder than words but often equally as loud. Do not berate them for their beliefs. Kindly and gently point out the errors in their teaching. Although tempted, do not attack them personally by telling them how stupid or prideful they are.

Never lose hope in the power of God. God keeps His promises. Very often, we do not see the small fissures forming in a rock that is constantly being pounded. Then after one more blow the rock breaks open. The word in Hebrew for rock also means stronghold. So God's word will deliver your loved ones from every stronghold entangling them.

Dear Father,

Please give me an awe and reverence for Your word. Teach me the value of Your word. Give me a greater understanding of who You are and the power of Your word.

Lord, You know the situation _____ is involved in. I ask You to show me scriptures to claim that will set him/her free. Help me to persevere and not lose heart. Help me to focus my eyes on You and not on the situation.

Thank You for hearing my prayer. Thank You for being a Father I can trust who will never disappoint me.

In Yeshua's (Jesus') name I pray,

Amen

ISRAEL

Israel – The Chosen People

Isaiah 14:1-3 *¹For the LORD will have mercy on Jacob, and will still choose Israel, and settle them in their own land. The strangers will be joined with them, and they will cling to the house of Jacob. ²Then people will take them and bring them to their place, and the house of Israel will possess them for servants and maids in the land of the LORD; they will take them captive whose captives they were, and rule over their oppressors.*

³It shall come to pass in the day the LORD gives you rest from your sorrow, and from your fear and the hard bondage in which you were made to serve.

Israel has never stopped being God's chosen people. Even though not all of Israel has chosen to follow the Messiah Yeshua (Jesus), God has not changed His mind. From the heathen nations of the earth, God separated the people of Israel and entrusted them with His word. He raised up kings and judges to lead and teach His people in the ways of righteousness.

He called Israel His special treasure, the apple of His eye. Even though He broke off some of the natural branches of the olive tree and grafted in branches from the wild olive tree He never entirely removed or forgot His chosen people Israel.

The words spoken by Isaiah, inspired by God, have not changed. **For the LORD will have mercy on Jacob, and will still choose Israel.** God's mercy is not conditional. God promises His mercy to fall on Israel. Israel has not stopped being chosen by God.

Some of God's promises have already been fulfilled in our lifetime. After years of homelessness, Israel has been **settled in**

their own land. Those who attempt to appropriate Israel's territory are fighting against God Himself.

The strangers will be joined with them, and they will cling to the house of Jacob. By the Hebrew definition, a stranger is one who does not have the same inherited rights as an Israeli. To cling means to attach or join themselves to Israel. In other words, strangers will follow the God of Israel as has happened in the church of today. However, too often the church has forgotten God's favor on Israel and has tried to usurp Israel's place.

The fulfillment of the latter part of this prophecy has not as yet come to pass. But we know it will. The Lord will judge those who are now threatening Israel and warring against her, killing innocent men, women and children. It is doubtful that seventy virgins will be awaiting the terrorists upon completion of their suicide missions.

Persecution, pogroms, anti-Semitism, hatred and prejudice throughout history including the present day have followed the Jewish people. But God promises that this will not last. **It shall come to pass in the day the LORD gives you rest from your sorrow, and from your fear and the hard bondage in which you were made to serve.** The Jewish people will not suffer forever.

Have you ever joined in anti-Semitic jokes?

Do you use clichés demeaning to Jewish people?

Do you feel, as a believer, you are superior to the Jews?

In the past, has your family been involved in persecution of the Jews?

Do you agree with the Palestinian view to drive Israel into the sea?

If your answers to any of the above questions have been 'yes' then perhaps you need an attitude adjustment.

Dear God of Abraham, Isaac and Jacob,

Forgive me for holding views or acting against Your chosen Jewish people. Teach me to love the Jewish people the way You do. I want to grow and change. I do not wish to remain the way I am. Change my thoughts and attitudes to line up with scripture.

Help me not to be arrogant toward the natural olive branches. Cleanse me from all unrighteousness. Give me a fuller understanding of Your ways. Bring Jewish people into my life so that I can bless them with Your love.

Thank You for teaching me Your love for the Jews.

In the name of the Prince of Peace, Yeshua the Messiah (Jesus Christ), the King of the Jews, I pray,

Amen

The God Of Second Chances

Ezekiel 11:16-20 *[16]Therefore say, 'Thus says the Lord GOD: "Although I have cast them far off among the Gentiles, and although I have scattered them among the countries, yet I shall be a little sanctuary for them in the countries where they have gone."' [17]Therefore say, 'Thus says the Lord GOD: "I will gather you from the peoples, assemble you from the countries where you have been scattered, and I will give you the land of Israel."' [18]And they will go there, and they will take away all its detestable things and all its abominations from there. [19]Then I will give them one heart, and I will put a new spirit within them, and take the stony heart out of their flesh, and give them a heart of flesh, [20]that they may walk in My statutes and keep My judgments and do them; and they shall be My people, and I will be their God.*

The fat lady never sings in God's kingdom. It may seem as if the final act is over and the curtain is closing but a new play is about to begin. We are so embedded in this world it becomes impossible to envision anything different. For that reason it is vital we constantly seek God's face through the Holy Scriptures.

How often did it appear the Jewish people were washed up, finished, beaten, and defeated? Yet, God never forgot His plan for them. God removed them from their familiar and comfortable surroundings and even separated them from each other. Then He sent them into foreign, unknown, and distant countries.

However, He never deserted them. He traveled with them. He suffered alongside of them. He became a protected place for them, **a little sanctuary,** where they could find respite from their hard labors. Nevertheless, God has times and seasons.

God promises to **gather the Jewish people from all the countries in which they have been scattered**. Not only will He reassemble them as a people **He will give them the land of Israel.**

God has accomplished this part of His promise. On May 14, 1948 Israel which had been dead to the world became alive again and an independent country where Jews from all over the world can become citizens.

Moreover, God's promise continues. God will cleanse His Jewish people from all unrighteousness and ungodliness. He will even give them a oneness and unity with Him. He **will give them one heart and a new spirit**.

Already that process has begun. Whenever an Israeli soldier is killed, sirens sound throughout the country. Everyone stops and the country observes a minute of silence. For that one moment they are one.

But God promises that oneness of heart will not last for merely one moment; it will last for eternity because they will all follow God's commandments.

If God can do miracles for Israel and the Jewish people then He can also do them for you.

Do you need a second chance in your life?

Do you find yourself separated from God?

Do you think there is no way you can extricate yourself from your situation?

Have you given up all hope?

There is an answer if you stop doing a few things and start doing others.

- ❖ Remove 'but' from your vocabulary, as in "But God I'm too old (too tired, too depressed, too sick, too poor, etc.).
- ❖ Stop giving yourself excuses.
- ❖ Stop focusing on everything that is wrong and out of order.
- ❖ Stop repeating all the lies the devil whispers in your ear.
- ❖ Stop blaming others for your situation.
- ❖ Stop complaining about your situation.

You can start doing other things.

- ❖ Start saying 'I can with God's help do …'
- ❖ Start taking responsibility for your own life.
- ❖ Start thanking God for everything good thing in your life no matter how small.
- ❖ Start speaking positive things. If you are unable to say anything positive then do not say anything.
- ❖ Start to forgive others who have done bad things to you.
- ❖ Start smiling instead of frowning.

Dear God,

I come to You in Yeshua's (Jesus') name expecting a miracle. I believe You can and will do a miracle for me because You love me. I see how You gave Israel a second chance and I know You can do the same for me. Help me to digest Your word in my heart and in my mind. Help me to depend on You and believe You. Help me to stop believing the lies of the enemy.

I will keep my eyes focused on You. Thank You for the results still unseen. Thank You for not giving up on me. Amen

The Land Of Israel

Jeremiah 23:7-8 *⁷"Therefore, behold, the days are coming," says the LORD, "that they shall no longer say, 'As the LORD lives who brought up the children of Israel from the land of Egypt,' ⁸but, 'As the LORD lives who brought up and led the descendants of the house of Israel from the north country and from all the countries where I had driven them.' And they shall dwell in their own land."*

After 400 years in bondage, God freed His people, Israel, from the tyranny of the Egyptians. He did it in a way that defied the logic of men. He raised up an eighty year old, dried up, hopeless sheep herder, reunited him with his family who he had not seen in sixty years and made him the deliverer of Israel.

His name was Moses. Even though he had been raised in the courts of Egypt he spent the majority of his life only among sheep and his immediate family. After an absence of sixty years, God thrusts him back in the royal court. This time Moses comes not in his own power but in the power of the Lord.

Pharaoh's deathlike grip on the Jewish people is only loosened by God's reign of miracles superior to all the conjurers in Egypt. Begrudgingly, after the death of his oldest son, Pharaoh agrees to allow the Jewish people to leave. However, he has second thoughts soon after their departure and sends a legion of chariots and horsemen to force them to return.

Moses, under God's leadership, performs the most spectacular miracle by dividing the Red Sea and allowing the Israelites to pass across on dry land and then drowning the Egyptians as they attempt to pursue them. Not only was this a lesson for the Egyptians it was also a powerful lesson for the Israelis.

Faced with the difficulties of the future in an unknown, dangerous land they could always bolster their faith by remembering God's deliverance. Jeremiah speaks of a second deliverance greater than the first. The exodus from Egypt will be eclipsed by the gathering of all those of Jewish descent from all the nations where they have been scattered for generations.

Moreover, **they shall dwell in their own land**. After the Holocaust, in May of 1948 Israel became an independent state. It was birthed in bloodshed as Britain, like Pharaoh, had difficulty removing her deathlike grip. However, the UN resolution allowed Israel her sovereignty.

Peace and tranquility have never been prevalent in Israel. Since her formation, her Arab neighbors have constantly tried to 'push her into the sea'. This small, arid parcel of land has been the hotspot in the Middle East for decades.

Why is it impossible for the Arabs to allow Israel to exist?

The answer is very simple. Israel has never stopped being God's chosen people. The devil hates God. Since he cannot hurt God, he chooses to hurt God's people instead. God calls Israel the apple of His eye. The devil keeps trying to poke out God's eye.

God is merciful and patient. Another meaning of patience is being slow to anger. For decades, God has allowed His people to be slaughtered by cowardly suicide bombers and hatemongers. The majority of the Jewish people do not live in Israel. Due to persecutions through the ages, they have been dispersed throughout the world.

God promises to bring all Jewish people back to Israel. The second exodus is beyond our imagination. Just as God moved in miraculous ways in the time of Moses He will do the same in our time.

Where do you stand in your support of Israel?

Do you want to stand on God's side?

Dear God of Abraham, Isaac and Jacob,

I come to You in the name of Yeshua (Jesus) the King of the Jews.

I ask You to forgive me for things I have said and thought against the Jewish people. I ask You to give me Your love for the Jewish people. Show me how to help those in Israel. Remind me to pray for Israel and the peace of Jerusalem.

Use me to help Your Jewish people.

Thank You Lord,

Amen

There Is None Like You

I Chronicles 17:20-22 ^{20}*O LORD, there is none like You, nor is there any God besides You, according to all that we have heard with our ears. ^{21}And who is like Your people Israel, the one nation on the earth whom God went to redeem for Himself as a people—to make for Yourself a name by great and awesome deeds, by driving out nations from before Your people whom You redeemed from Egypt? ^{22}For You have made Your people Israel Your very own people forever; and You, LORD, have become their God.*

King David spoke these words to the Lord after Nathan, the prophet, reported his vision in I Chronicles 17:4-12. Nathan's vision included several points:

a) David was not allowed to build a house for the Lord to live in.
b) The Lord will give the Jewish people their own land
c) The Lord will establish Israel
d) The Jewish people will not have to leave the land of Israel
e) The Jewish people will not be oppressed as they were before
f) The Lord will build a house for David (establish the kingship of David's family forever)

The nature of God is clearly illustrated in this exchange between David and the Lord. God begins by telling David he is not allowed to build a house for Him and ends by telling him He will build a house for David. In addition, God answers David's cry for his people by establishing them in their own land.

There are many who wish to throw Israel into the sea. Modern day Israel is very small compared to Biblical Israel. Yet Israel's neighbors still complain. The terrorism aimed at Israel is really aimed at God. According to God's word, the land of Israel belongs to the Jewish people. God's word does not change. Israel is here to stay.

When the Lord says He will build a house for David He is referring to the Messiah who comes from the lineage of David. The Messiah, Yeshua (Jesus), is firmly established on the throne forever. Whether or not people believe in Yeshua does not negate His kingship over all the earth.

David's reaction to the Lord's word is a model we need to emulate. David's heart is bursting with love for the Lord. In those days, as it still is today, many distractions pull at a person's heart. However, David was single mindedly devoted to the Lord. He did not allow himself to be seduced into worshiping anything or anyone except God alone.

As the ruler of Israel, David's main concern was for his people. God promises David, and all of posterity that He will establish His throne forever. For thousands of years, civilizations have been birthed then died but Israel is alive again as God fulfills His promise to David. **You have made Your people Israel Your very own people forever; and You, LORD, have become their God.**

The Jewish people belong to the Lord because He has chosen them. No doctrine, theology, foreign government or resolution can separate them from their God. The Lord has set His favor upon Israel and as believers we should do the same.

Do we hold bitterness against Israel or the Jewish people? It does not matter if we are Jew or gentile because anti-Semitism attacks both groups of people.

Do we stereotype Jews?
Do we make ethnic jokes against Jews?
In past generations, have some in our family persecuted the Jews?
Do we believe the incorrect teaching that the church is Israel?
Do we claim Biblical promises reserved for Israel alone as our own?
Have we taught incorrect doctrine concerning Israel?
Do we love Israel and the Jewish people the way God does?

If you want your heart to line up with God's heart concerning the Jewish people then pray this prayer.

Dear Lord,

I come to You in the name of Your son, Yeshua, who sits on the throne with You forever. In examining my belief system I find it does not line up with Your word. I desire a greater closeness with You.

I ask You to teach me the truth concerning the Jewish people and Israel. I ask You to confirm Your word in me.

Forgive me for making jokes about Jews. Forgive me for using expressions demeaning to Jews.

I stand in for my relatives who in the past persecuted the Jews. I ask forgiveness for their actions. I break any unholy generational bonds over my family and myself.

I ask You to forgive me for following or teaching incorrect doctrine concerning Israel and the Jewish people.

I know Israel and the Jewish people are important to You and I want them to be important to me as well. I ask You to expand my heart so I can love Israel and the Jewish people the way God does.

Thank You Lord, Amen

SEPARATION FROM GOD

Which Is Better Strength Or Weakness?

2 Chronicles 26:16 *¹⁶But when he was strong his heart was lifted up, to his destruction, for he transgressed against the LORD his God by entering the temple of the LORD to burn incense on the altar of incense.*

When Uzziah was sixteen years old, he ascended to the throne of Judah. At that time, his father, King Amaziah, was murdered for turning away from the Lord and leading the country into defeat.

King Uzziah attempted to learn from his father's mistakes. At first he sought the Lord and received visions. Under God's inspiration Uzziah invented weapons of warfare hundreds of years ahead of their time. Judah enjoyed great military victories. Uzziah's fame spread throughout the world.

However, once he became powerful his arrogance led to his downfall. It was the sacred duty of the priests alone to burn incense to the Lord; however, Uzziah decided to **enter the temple** to perform this ritual. The priests angrily confronted him. Before their very eyes, the Lord struck King Uzziah with leprosy on his forehead.

Lepers were considered unclean. Not only were they unable to serve in the temple but also they had to be separated from the general population because leprosy was contagious. For the rest of Uzziah's life he was forced to remain in isolation apart from everyone.

What causes a person to become separated from the Lord?

At the impressionable age of sixteen Uzziah's father, Amaziah is murdered for disobeying the Lord. Amaziah defeated Seir, seized their idols, established them in his kingdom and proceeded to bow down to them. The prophet of God said to him, "Why have you sought the gods of the people, which could not rescue their own people from your hand?" (2 Chronicles 25:15)

This stupidity and irrational thinking is handed down from father to son.

Are we so different from Amaziah and Uzziah? Replace 'they' and 'them' with your name or someone you know.

- ❖ When *they* were weak, *they* followed the Lord.
- ❖ The Lord blessed *them* for their obedience.
- ❖ Once *they* were strong, *they* deserted the Lord.
- ❖ The Lord removed *them* from leadership.
- ❖ The Lord punished *them*.

What causes us to lean on the Lord when we are weak but desert Him when we are strong?

Perhaps it is because we enthrone self. How can we bow down and worship God when we are so enamored with self?

After we achieve a certain measure of success in this world, we begin to forget who was responsible for that success. We listen to our colleagues who tickle our ears with words of praise. We stop listening to the steady voice of God who has guided us through tumultuous times and instead listen to sycophants who murmur sweet sayings. Our focus shifts to ourselves. We try to perceive ourselves the way others see us instead of the way the Lord sees us. We forget to focus Him.

Has your focus shifted? Do you want God to be the center of your attention? If so then pray this prayer.

Dear Lord,

You know I have strayed from worshiping You. My initial zeal is gone. Your word seems dry and lifeless to me. I only think about You when I go to services. Then I quickly forget You again.

I do not want to continue existing like this. There is something missing from my life. It is You. I want You back in the center of my life and in the center of my heart.

I ask You to forgive me for placing _____ on the throne in my life. Help me to change.

Thank You for hearing and answering my prayer. I am expecting and welcome a change in my life.

In Yeshua's (Jesus') name I pray,

Amen

Return From The Diaspora

Ezra 3:12-13 *¹²But many of the priests and Levites and heads of the fathers' houses, old men who had seen the first temple, wept with a loud voice when the foundation of this temple was laid before their eyes. Yet many shouted aloud for joy, ¹³so that the people could not discern the noise of the shout of joy from the noise of the weeping of the people, for the people shouted with a loud shout, and the sound was heard afar off.*

For seventy years the Jewish people were exiled from their land. They had been carried off to Babylon and forced to stay there. Later on, Babylon was conquered by Cyrus of Persia. God spoke to Cyrus, a pagan, concerning the return of the Jewish people to Jerusalem, which fulfilled the prophecy of Jeremiah.

Cyrus proclaimed the Jewish people were to return to Jerusalem to rebuild the temple of Solomon, which had been destroyed. In addition, he commanded his subjects to give the Jews gold, silver, livestock and a freewill offering for the rebuilding of the temple in Jerusalem. Cyrus returned items plundered from the original temple.

When the foundation of the new temple was laid, there was a mixture of emotion. **The people could not discern the noise of the shout of joy from the noise of the weeping of the people, for the people shouted with a loud shout, and the sound was heard afar off.**

The elderly, who were over seventy years old, remembered the glory of Solomon's temple as well as being overcome with finally returning home. Heartfelt weeping exploded from their innermost being. Simultaneously, the younger generation who had grown up in Babylon experienced great joy at the laying of the temple's foundation and the anticipation of a new life.

The intermingling of the sounds covered every gamut of emotion. Even those who were distant from the construction site heard and wondered at the diverse sound of mourning intermixed with rejoicing.

For seventy years, the Jews were in the Diaspora being strangers in a strange land unable to worship God in His temple.

Do you feel that way?

Are you estranged from the Lord?

Are you held captive not by a foreign people but by addiction, false teaching or spiritual laziness?

Do you want to come home again?

Do you want to experience God's presence?

Did you have a strong walk with the Lord, at one time, but now you cannot even find the pathway?

Does your spiritual life need to be reinvigorated?

The Jewish people used cedar logs for building materials. Your building materials could consist of:

- ❖ Reading the Bible on a daily basis
- ❖ Claiming Bible promises for your life and those you care for
- ❖ Thanking God for choosing you as His child
- ❖ Shifting your focus from yourself to others
- ❖ Singing praises to God
- ❖ Associating with people who love God

- ❖ Removing things from your life that pull you away from God
- ❖ Breaking unhealthy relationships

You can pray these things into your life.

Dear Father,

I have been separate from You for a long time. My heart hurts missing our past relationship. I renounce _____ and everything that divides me from You. I give You permission to remove these harmful things, whether they are relationships, habits and/or addictions, from my life.

I ask You to teach me healthy ways to live my life that will restore me to Yourself. Show me anything else in my life You find unholy and unhealthy. I place myself in Your hands. I desire to obey You and follow You all the days of my life.

Help me experience once again the joy of knowing and walking with You. Let my life be like the shouting of the Jewish people heard at a great distance. Let others wonder at the change in my life.

I am so grateful to You, my Father and my King, that You hear my prayer. I am expecting a new beginning, a return from my Diaspora.

In the name of Your son, Yeshua (Jesus) I pray,

Amen

Getting Off Track

1 Chronicles 10:13-14 *[13]So Saul died for his unfaithfulness which he had committed against the LORD, because he did not keep the word of the LORD, and also because he consulted a medium for guidance. [14]But he did not inquire of the LORD; therefore He killed him, and turned the kingdom over to David the son of Jesse.*

Getting off track is the story of Saul the Benjamite, a.k.a. King Saul, the first king of Israel. Saul was hand picked by God to lead Israel. Samuel, the prophet anointed him king and observed how Saul stood head and shoulders above the rest.

Unfortunately, he only stood head and shoulders taller in stature not in Godly obedience. Saul killed himself on the battlefield but God says he **died for his unfaithfulness**. The Hebrew word for unfaithfulness is מַעַל (ma al) and its fuller meaning is treachery, sin, and transgression.

Saul committed this treachery not against a man but against God Himself. He committed this treachery in several ways.

- ❖ **He did not keep the word of the LORD.** Word in Hebrew is דָּבָר (da var) and means a word, commandment, decree, judgment, or message of the Lord. Many times Saul ignored God's commandment: he assumed priestly responsibilities at Amalek, did not wait for Samuel but sacrificed to the Lord himself, did not totally destroy enemies but kept the plunder, and killed innocent priests at Nob during his crazed search for David.
- ❖ **He consulted a medium for guidance.** By Saul's decree, in obedience to the Lord, all mediums and spiritists were forced to leave. Saul was aware there was a

medium at En Dor who covertly conducted séances with the dead. (Interestingly, even though he knew of her existence he never killed her for breaking the law.) Now he perceives his situation as desperate ("I am deeply distressed; for the Philistines make war against me, and God has departed from me and does not answer me anymore, neither by prophets nor by dreams." 1 Samuel 28:7) So he calls up Samuel from the dead.

❖ **But he did not inquire of the LORD.** Saul never developed his own relationship with the Lord. He put his hope and trust in Samuel. Even though Samuel was an effective prophet, he was still a man. Men die; men disappoint us; men sin. God is perfect in all ways. God was not pleased Saul had never taken the time or effort to know Him.

Is your life on the right track or have you gotten derailed?

Are you in a desperate situation?

Are you not hearing from God?

Are you searching for answers in biblically gray areas because your pain is so great?

Do you pray to angels to help you instead of God alone?

Do you listen to men instead of God?

Do you call the psychic hotline for fun?

Have you ever had your palm read, handwriting analyzed, or horoscope cast?

Have you ever had your tea leaves read?

Do you wear power bracelets, crystals, ankhs or amulets?

Do you consult the Kabala?

Do you play with the Ouija Board, Super 8 Ball or Tarot cards?

Do you consult the I Ching?

Do you want to get right with God?

Saul never asked God to forgive him. You have that chance. If you want God's forgiveness and blessing in your life then pray this prayer.

Dear Heavenly Father,

I come to You in all humbleness. I have broken Your laws. I have _____ (list the things you have done that are not pleasing to God.) I know these things are wrong. I do not want to have any open doors in my life, which give entrance to the enemy.

I dedicate my life to serving You. I want all pagan influences out of my life, mind and heart. I want You to lead me all the days of my life. I ask You to show me books, videos and music which I own that are an abomination to You. I want to remove everything unpleasing to You from my house.

I ask You, Lord, to renew, restore and refresh areas in my life taken over by the evil one. Teach me Your ways. Warn me if I begin to get off track.

I receive Your forgiveness.

Thank You Lord for never leaving me or forsaking me even though I stray from You.

In Yeshua's (Jesus') name,

Amen

Finding God

Jeremiah 50:4-5 *[4] "In those days and in that time," says the
LORD,*
"The children of Israel shall come,
They and the children of Judah together;
With continual weeping they shall come,
And seek the LORD their God.
[5] They shall ask the way to Zion,
With their faces toward it, saying,
'Come and let us join ourselves to the LORD
In a perpetual covenant
That will not be forgotten.'

Is God lost? Obviously not, we are the ones who have taken a wrong turn and gotten off the path of righteousness. Very often, we are busy with the cares and concerns of life ranging from how to schedule three conflicting soccer games to wondering how we will make the mortgage payment and everything in between.

It seems as if every minute of our day is filled with something to do or somewhere to go. Sometimes there is not a moment to sit down and enter into the presence of the Lord. Sometimes we choose not to. Sometimes we purposely program ourselves so there are no gaps. Sometimes we do not choose to hear what the Lord might say to us. Sometimes we glance at our surroundings and are shocked to see how far we have strayed.

God does not leave us floundering in treacherous places. He always provides a means of escape. That escape leads us directly into His everlasting arms always waiting to embrace us.

The event precipitating our return forces us to see clearly where we have been and where we are headed. Weeping may spring up from deep places in our innermost being. Sometimes there will be no words or thoughts but only deep grief at our separation from our Father.

We seek once again to enter into God's presence. We promise not to forget Him and relegate Him to an unused part of our life. But will He accept us?

The answer is, yes. He never leaves us. We leave Him. No matter how far we wander from Him He always remembers His **perpetual covenant** to us.

When you look at your life, are you surprised at what you see? Have you drifted off the road?

Is there an emptiness inside you that can only be filled by your Creator?

The first step to getting back on track is realizing you are lost. The second step is talking to your Heavenly Father. The third step is following His direction.

Dear Heavenly Father,

I am lost. Great emptiness surrounds me. No matter what I do, this sadness always remains with me. I come into Your Presence and ask for Your forgiveness.

Take me back to Your side. Hold me close. Teach me where I have gone wrong and how to correct my bad decisions. Help me to stop thinking about things that are unprofitable and harmful to me.

I give you permission to move in my life and change things. I do not want to remain where I am. I ask You to touch me now and join me to Yourself.

In Yeshua's (Jesus') name I pray, Amen

Return And Be Healed

Jeremiah 3:20-22 *²⁰ Surely, as a wife treacherously departs from her husband,*
So have you dealt treacherously with Me,
O house of Israel," says the LORD.
²¹ A voice was heard on the desolate heights,
Weeping and supplications of the children of Israel.
For they have perverted their way;
They have forgotten the LORD their God.
²² "Return, you backsliding children,
And I will heal your backslidings."

At times, we have all turned away from God. The powerful lure of other things have pulled us away from the one true God. For some the promise of self-calming peace has led them to reject the God of their fathers. For others the glamour and riches of this world have led them to refuse to allow God in their lives. They may give Him lip service but their service goes no further than their lips. In addition, for others the allure of satanic spiritual power has led them astray.

Following the Lord takes courage. Many are estranged from parents, coworkers, friends and teachers. Standing with the Lord at times entails standing alone. The popular path is not always the holy path.

In this passage from Jeremiah, the Lord compares us to His wife. He has exalted us to a position of being dearly beloved by Him. However, how have we treated Him? We have treated Him treacherously.

The Hebrew word is בָּגַד (ba gad) and means to act covertly, to pillage, deal deceitfully, to deal treacherously, to deal unfaithfully, to offend, to transgress, to depart, and to be unfaithful.

Have you done any of these things? Do you profess to give your heart to Yeshua (Jesus) but covertly set your affections elsewhere? Are you unfaithful, dabbling in Buddhism, Scientology, Yoga, and/or American Indian worship? Yet you still proclaim yourself a believer?

The answer for the vast number of believers is yes. At times, we have all held divided hearts toward God. Wrong teachings, the attraction of forbidden pleasures and/or self-absorption have turned us away from following God.

When catastrophes and disasters strike, all our superficial attachments are valueless. Those closely held false teachings are worthless in the face of tragedy. There is only One who can save us. His name is Yeshua, (Jesus) and He calls to us to return to Him.

We need to examine our hearts before calamity strikes and confirm we are in right relationship with the Lord our Creator. Have our affections gone astray? Do we read God's word on a regular basis and learn from it. The key is not only reading God's word but also gaining knowledge of God and insight into ourselves.

God stands with open arms asking us to return to Him. If we do not walk toward Him, we will never receive His forgiveness. If there is a lack of closeness to God in your life then pray this prayer.

Dear Father,

Forgive me for forsaking You. I have been drawn away from You but I wish to return. You promise to heal my backsliding. I desire to be healed by You. I have suffered many wounds by those who call themselves believers. Instead of blaming them, I have blamed You. I understand now that You are not to blame. Forgive me for drawing away from You.

I ask You to draw me close once again. I desire to feel Your presence. I desire Your hand to guide me as I make decisions. Help me to be faithful to You. Show me when I begin to wander away from You.

I proclaim today _____ (write in the date) as a new beginning in my life.

In Yeshua's (Jesus') name I pray,

Amen

TESTING AND TRIALS

The Battle Is The Lord's

I Samuel 17:46-47 *⁴⁶This day the LORD will deliver you into my hand, and I will strike you and take your head from you. And this day I will give the carcasses of the camp of the Philistines to the birds of the air and the wild beasts of the earth, that all the earth may know that there is a God in Israel. ⁴⁷Then all this assembly shall know that the LORD does not save with sword and spear; for the battle is the LORD'S, and He will give you into our hands."*

When David faced Goliath, he had a giant battle on his hands. Very often our battles can loom as large as giants in our minds. In anticipation, we foresee every thing that can go wrong. In our mind's eye, in full Technicolor, we are beaten before the battle even begins.

Sometimes we are being realists. We know we are out of our league and beyond our level of expertise. All our friends tell us we are silly, or worse yet, wrong to pursue a battle seemingly impossible to win. But why do we persevere?

Because the battle really is the Lord's.

Before we become hasty in claiming the victory there are a few ground rules we need to observe. When David had his confrontation with Goliath, Samuel had already anointed him king. God had chosen David because he was a young man after God's own heart. In other words, God was first in David's life.

Is God first in your life?

David focused his attention on the Lord. The taunts and threats spewing out of Goliath's mouth did not find fertile ground to grow in David's mind. His mind was overflowing with the power and glory of God Almighty. David did not think it was David versus Goliath but rather it was The Lord Of Hosts versus Goliath.

In your battles focus on God's strength not your own weakness.

Saul tried to equip David properly for the battle. Generously, he offered him his own armor. David tried it on but realized it was not his style. He could not pretend to be someone he was not.

Are you trying to fight your battle using someone else's style?

David used unorthodox weapons of warfare. Five, smooth, white stones did not compare equally with a 15 pound javelin and 125 pounds of armor; not to mention the shield a special shield bearer had to carry. However, David was familiar with his stones and slingshot. He already had a successful track record with killing a lion and a bear that attacked his father's sheep.

Use weapons with which you are familiar: prayer, fasting, a multitude of wise counselors, seeking the Lord's will, and waiting on the Lord.

David knew this fight was not against him, Saul, or Israel but it was against the Lord.

Do not claim the battle as your own. Leave it in the Lord's hands.

David knew God would deliver Goliath into his hands.

Believe God will deliver your enemy into your hands.

Dear Father,

Thank You for the victory I have in You. Thank You for being God Almighty – not HalfMighty or AlmostMighty but Almighty. There is no power in Heaven or Earth that can stand against You.

I will not dwell on the enemy or the threats he has made against me. I will keep my mind focused on You and on Your promises in Your word. I will not shrink back or be afraid. I will face the enemy using Your weapons of warfare and not his.

I release the weight of the battle that is bearing down on me into Your hands. I will stop personalizing the battle and acknowledge it is Your battle and not my own. I will not claim it as mine.

I am thanking You in advance for the great victory.

In Yeshua's (Jesus') name,

Amen

Mining For Gold

Job 23:8-12 *⁸ "Look, I go forward, but He is not there,
And backward, but I cannot perceive Him;
⁹ When He works on the left hand, I cannot behold Him;
When He turns to the right hand, I cannot see Him.
¹⁰ But He knows the way that I take;
When He has tested me, I shall come forth as gold.
¹¹ My foot has held fast to His steps;
I have kept His way and not turned aside.
¹² I have not departed from the commandment of His lips;
I have treasured the words of His mouth
More than my necessary food.*

God is mining for gold. We are the precious metal He is harvesting. Deposits of gold are found in rivers. In its natural state gold is encrusted with worthless ore. Strong jets of water are directed at the ore to separate the gold. Gold is so valuable even mining for a tiny speck in a large chunk of ore is worthwhile.

God sees our lives as precious to Him. Even when we are encrusted with every type of filth, He can see through to that golden speck. The hard part is extricating the golden ore. God's method of mining is called testing.

In a testing situation, Job's words ring true in our hearts. We go forward with a situation but *it may seem as if* we are going alone, as if He is not there. If we try to tackle the situation a different way and look for God, again *it may seem as if* He is not there. It does not matter which way we turn, *it always may seem as if* He is not there.

We can learn from Job's example. Perception and reality are two different things. God is not unaware or asleep concerning our situation. He realizes what is happening. Often we do not comprehend we are in the miner's pan. He is washing us with water to remove the gold from the worthless ore. And it is difficult.

By nature, we cling to worthless thought patterns, habits and relationships. Only the terrible time of testing forces us to leave valueless things behind. The testing process will end. At that time, we, like Job, will come forth like gold.

During this time of testing, we are to remain reading and applying God's word to our lives. We are to continue following God's commandments and value God's word even greater than earthly food.

How do we do this?

One way is through prayer. We let God know we are mindful of His promises and have faith in His word. Tests begin and end. We need to remember His word will come to fruition and there will be an end to our testing. When it comes, we too will shine forth like precious gold.

Dear Father,

I am in the midst of a difficult situation now. I believe the words of Job. I too feel as if You are not near me. But I know this is a testing time. I know You are aware of my situation. I know that times of testing are for my good.

I know it is Your desire that I come forth like gold.

I desire to change. I will no longer hold on to unhealthy thoughts, habits and relationships. I seek Your guidance.

I thank You for the work You are doing in my life even though it is very painful right now. I know this time will end and then I like Job will declare I have come forth like gold.

I anticipate Your restorative power in my life.

Thank You for caring and loving me enough to bother to cleanse me.

In Yeshua's (Jesus') name,

Amen

His Name Is Wonderful

Judges 13:17-20 *[17]Then Manoah said to the Angel of the LORD, "What is Your name, that when Your words come to pass we may honor You?"*

[18]And the Angel of the LORD said to him, "Why do you ask My name, seeing it is wonderful?"

[19]So Manoah took the young goat with the grain offering, and offered it upon the rock to the LORD. And He did a wondrous thing while Manoah and his wife looked on—[20]it happened as the flame went up toward heaven from the altar—the Angel of the LORD ascended in the flame of the altar!

Dark times covered the land of the Israelites. For forty years they were under the cruel control of the Philistines. Even though the Israelites had not walked correctly in all their ways God still heard their cry. He heard the corporate and individual prayer in their hearts and on their lips.

He sent The Angel of the Lord (some believe Him to be the preincarnate Messiah) twice to the barren wife of Manoah. The Angel promised her that her son would redeem Israel from the hand of the Philistines.

Manoah had difficulty believing his wife's account. It was not logical. God's graciousness not only allowed The Angel to appear to Manoah's wife a second time but also allowed Him to wait while she ran to get her husband. Even with The Angel in front of him Manoah still could not trust.

The Angel not only said His name was Wonderful but demonstrated it by performing a wondrous feat. He ascended into heaven within the flame of the altar. Finally, Manoah believed.

Do you need something wonderful in your life? Is there a long standing, unresolved issue to which you have devoted much prayer?

If so, then stand on this promise. If God answered the cry of the Israelites and Manoah's wife then He can answer yours.

Claim this word as your own. God tells us His name is Wonderful. Names in the Old Testament described someone's character. Since God's name is Wonderful He will do **wondrous** feats in your life. God is no respecter of persons. He will do various wondrous things for all who call on His name

Stop languishing in the depths of despair. God is faithful. He will keep His promises. Talk to your Father and your God.

Dear Father,

Forgive me for only seeing the problem. I know You are Wonderful and can do wondrous things in my life and my family's lives. I believe You can take my hopeless situation and turn it around. I know it would take a miracle. But You are the creator of miracles. I ask You to perform a miracle in my life.

You heard the cry of Manoah's wife; I know You hear my cry. I ask You Lord to move actively in my situation. (Insert your prayer request to the Lord.) Just like The Angel of the Lord showed Manoah something totally unexpected and wondrous I ask You to do the same for me.

Forgive me if I have dictated solutions for my problem to You. I want Your answer to my dilemma. I choose Your ways over my ways and the world's ways. I give You permission to change my life. I release all my cares and concerns to You. Thank you Lord for being a God and Father who hears and cares.

In the name of Your Son, Yeshua (Jesus), I pray, Amen

Passing The Test

2 Chronicles 32:31 *[31]However, regarding the ambassadors of the princes of Babylon, whom they sent to him to inquire about the wonder that was done in the land, God withdrew from him, in order to test him, that He might know all that was in his heart.*

King Hezekiah is remembered for restoring the sanctity of the temple and the worship of God. He unified Judah and destroyed the altars and high places where the people had worshiped pagan gods. God blessed Hezekiah and the Jewish people with peace. He also inspired Hezekiah to build a series of aqueducts that brought water into the city of Jerusalem.

Even though Hezekiah was of the lineage of David, his father and grandfather had been poor role models. Hezekiah alone stood as a paragon of godliness in an ungodly world.

But what happened?

In the later years of his reign, ambassadors from the country of Babylon came to observe the wonders (another meaning is miracles and signs) that were done in the land.

Hezekiah had a choice. On one hand, he showed the ambassadors everything from soup to nuts. But he never gave credit to the Cook. Self pride was enthroned in Hezekiah's heart.

We discover this was part of God's plan. We are told **God withdrew from him**. The Hebrew word for withdrew is עָזַב (ahs zav) and also means to loosen. God loosens His hold on Hezekiah's heart so He can determine Hezekiah's true feelings.

God had walked step by step with Hezekiah, encouraging, guiding, and leading him on the path of righteousness. He had also been teaching him. This time of testing comes at the end of Hezekiah's life. God expects us to retain the things we have spent a lifetime learning. Hezekiah flunked his test.

He forgot who was responsible for all the prosperity, peace and world acclaim. He listened to the voices of flatterers extolling his virtues. When ambassadors came from as far away as Babylon, he gloried in their adulation. The more they praised him the more he had to show them.

But in God's mercy Hezekiah was not killed or even dethroned. He was told by the prophet Isaiah, all his treasures, of which he was so proud, would be carried off to Babylon and some of his sons would become eunuchs in the Babylonian king's palace.

There are consequences in not learning our lessons and failing God's test. How do you think you would score?

One way to be assured of passing is by keeping your focus on God. When God does great things in your life never forget your author and perfecter. Never confuse ministering *for* the Lord with ministering *to* the Lord. Keep your ears tuned to God's frequency, not man's.

Dear Father,

I know You are a kind and gracious God. I ask You to impress my mind and heart with the lessons You have taught me. I want to pass Your test. Help me to always keep my heart humble. Help me to remember to keep my priorities straight. May You always be number one in my life.

In Yeshua's (Jesus') name, Amen

Our Deceitful Hearts

Jeremiah 17:9-10 *[9]"The heart is deceitful above all things, And desperately wicked; Who can know it? [10] I, the LORD, search the heart, I test the mind, Even to give every man according to his ways, According to the fruit of his doings.*

A certain Messianic Rabbi was a strong and moral leader of his congregation. He taught with a kind and compassionate heart the full meaning of the scriptures and yet, for a time, this was his favorite verse. For his birthday, one year, his congregation presented him with a cake using this verse as the inscription. He literally ate and digested God's word.

God is speaking this scripture to everyone on this earth with no exceptions. The heart is the seat of our feelings. Circumstances, half-truths, and our imaginations all play a part in coloring and shading facts. Our feelings are untrustworthy. At times, they are true but at other times false. Acting on feelings alone will never produce consistent fruit.

To understand the meaning better we examine the Hebrew. The Hebrew word for wicked is אָנַשׁ (ah nash), and means to be frail, feeble, melancholy, incurable, sick, or woeful. At times, our hearts experience this. Regardless of the confident, self-assured appearance we present to the world there is a place of weakness in all of us.

God is emphasizing our heart is not to be solely relied upon. The heart is impossible to be fully understood. It is the core of our emotions. For most of us, as we age and mature, the oscillations of our heart decrease. Our feelings become more stable and less unpredictable.

God searches our hearts. The Hebrew word for search is חקר (ha kar) and the full meaning is to penetrate, to examine intimately, find out, as well as search. God delves deeper than any cardiologist does. He listens to every murmur, gurgle and sigh. Not only does He listen He also understands.

He tests our minds. He investigates, examines and tries our minds attempting to discover our essential motivations. He does these things for a reason. God is a rewarder of those who walk in His ways and follow His path.

What is the state of your heart?

Are you prepared for an intensive investigation of your most private feelings?

Do you have a divided heart?

Do you desire God to cleanse your heart of everything He finds objectionable?

Dear Holy Father,

I come to You in the name of Your Son Yeshua (Jesus). I desire to walk correctly in all Your ways. I want to honor You with my life.

I ask You to search my heart. If there is anything that is not right I ask You to show it to me. Help me to overcome thoughts related to feelings that are not holy or Godly. Deliver me from the temptations of this world.

Help me to not be swept away by the depth of my emotions. Keep my feet on the stable ground of Your word. I ask for Your Holy Spirit, the Ruach HaKodesh to help me to discern truth from falsehood.

Thank You for being a God who helps me to mature, grow, and not remain a child.

Amen

Restoration

Job 42:10-17 *¹⁰And the LORD restored Job's losses when he prayed for his friends. Indeed the LORD gave Job twice as much as he had before. ¹¹Then all his brothers, all his sisters, and all those who had been his acquaintances before, came to him and ate food with him in his house; and they consoled him and comforted him for all the adversity that the LORD had brought upon him. Each one gave him a piece of silver and each a ring of gold.*

¹²Now the LORD blessed the latter days of Job more than his beginning; for he had fourteen thousand sheep, six thousand camels, one thousand yoke of oxen, and one thousand female donkeys. ¹³He also had seven sons and three daughters. ¹⁴And he called the name of the first Jemimah, the name of the second Keziah, and the name of the third Keren-Happuch. ¹⁵In all the land were found no women so beautiful as the daughters of Job; and their father gave them an inheritance among their brothers.

¹⁶After this Job lived one hundred and forty years, and saw his children and grandchildren for four generations. ¹⁷So Job died, old and full of days.

In the midst of trials and tribulations, you need to raise your eyes to the Lord and see how He has dealt with others. No one can deny Job could be the poster boy for troubles in life. He lost his children, his possessions, his friends, his social standing and the sympathy of his wife.

Testing will end. It seems as if it will last forever but that is a lie from the devil. During times of testing there may be people who have not treated us as kindly as we would expect. A tendency of human nature is to desire retaliation for past abuses. It is extremely interesting to note God restored Job's losses once he prayed for his friends. In order to pray sincerely for someone you need to forgive him or her. God is telling us to forgive those who wronged us so that we receive full restoration.

God also dealt with the friends. They were required to offer seven bulls and seven rams as a burnt offering. They knew it was God's requirement for Job to pray for them.

When God restores He gives us more than we possessed in the beginning. Formerly, Job was a man of great wealth; he lost it all. God restored double to him. He had an additional ten children after ten of his children died. His three daughters were very beautiful and he took the unusual step in those days, of awarding them an inheritance along with their brothers.

Job was not young when his trials began but God added one hundred and forty years to his life. He gave him a double lifetime. He became a great-great-grandfather before he died. The expression **full of days** implies not only that he lived a long life but also it was a full and content life. The Hebrew word for full is שָׂבֵעַ (sa vay) and means filled to satisfaction.

God will get you through your trial and you too will be filled to satisfaction. Raise your eyes to the Lord and expect your deliverance.

Dear Father,

I lift my eyes to You. All my hope is in You. You know the circumstances of my life. I ask You to help me to forgive those who have wronged and maligned me. There are bitter wounds in my heart. I ask You to heal them and help me to move on. I do not want to be stuck in despair and despondency.

You are my healer. I accept Your healing. I look forward with keen anticipation, to the day of my deliverance and full resto-

ration. You are a faithful God and I know because You did it for Job You will do it for me.

I hold on to Job's promise that he died old and full of days. I claim that as my own. Premature death will not overtake me. Poverty will not overtake me. I will live a long time and declare the glory of You Lord.

Thank You for being a wonderful God,

In Yeshua's (Jesus') name I pray,

Amen

TRAGEDIES

Turning Weakness Into Strength

Isaiah 40:29-31 *²⁹He gives power to the weak,
And to those who have no might He increases strength.
³⁰ Even the youths shall faint and be weary,
And the young men shall utterly fall,
³¹ But those who wait on the LORD
Shall renew their strength;
They shall mount up with wings like eagles,
They shall run and not be weary,
They shall walk and not faint.*

It does not matter if we can bench press 400 pounds there are still some situations in which we are weak.

It does not matter if we are a CEO (chief executive officer) of a Fortune 500 company there are still some situations in which we are weak.

It does not matter if we have an IQ of 200 there are still some situations in which we are weak.

There are bone-crushing circumstances that befall the strongest, the best and the brightest. Our only hope for overcoming the trials and tribulations of this world is through the Lord.

He promises us power when we are weak. In fact, He further states even if **we have no might** He increases strength. Even at a time when **youths shall faint and be weary** we will still be strengthened. The Lord expands on this thought. We will be strengthened even though **the young men shall utterly** (totally) **fall.**

There is one condition. We need to **wait on the Lord**. Our weak condition may persist for a time as we wait. However, we are not to lose hope. God's promise is that He will renew our strength. In fact, we will soar above our problems with **wings like eagles**. We will run our race; complete our task no matter how difficult, without being weary. We shall walk and not collapse.

This scripture portion is discussing times in our lives when we are about to admit defeat. We have wrestled with problems and situations in our lives and in the lives of our families and we know we cannot win. We are correct. By ourselves, we cannot gain the victory.

We need supernatural solutions for overwhelming, deeply entrenched problems. The answer does not always come as soon as we would desire. The key elements are waiting, expecting, hoping in the Lord. Our eyes need to be focused on Him and not on our problems.

We can do several things as we wait:

- Thank Him for answers not yet received
- Try and help others in more desperate situations than our own
- Repeat God's promises to Him
- Remember all the past victories and battles the Lord has brought us through
- Associate with people who edify and encourage us
- Do not voice our fears about the situation
- Do not let minor setbacks demoralize us
- Stay in the word of God

Dear Father,

I am very weak. Only You know the full extent of my situation. Only You realize all I have suffered. I feel as though I cannot fight one more battle. I am totally relying on You to fight for me. I need You to turn my weakness into Your strength. Only through Your intervention can I soar above this problem.

I am looking to You for my deliverance. If there is anything I am doing that is incorrect, I ask You to correct me. I desire a teachable spirit. In the past, You have done wonderful things in my life. I ask You to do it again.

I thank You in advance. Even though I do not see the victory, I believe I will gain it through You. This situation is extremely difficult for me but easy for You. I release all my cares, concerns, worries and disappointments to You.

In Yeshua's (Jesus') name I pray,

Amen

Deadly Situations

2 Kings 4:40 *⁴⁰Now it happened, as they were eating the stew, that they cried out and said, "Man of God, there is death in the pot!"*

Elisha is with the sons of prophets and they are hungry. There is a famine in the land and no one has sufficient food. Elisha instructs them to start boiling water in anticipation of the stew they are going to eat.

A prophet gathers herbs and gourds from a wild vine. They had never eaten those gourds before. When the stew is ready one of the prophets tastes it and cries out, **"Man of God, there is death in the pot!"**

He did not say someone had already died. The implication of the statement is if they eat it someone will die.

They are in a deadly situation. The stew is their only available food. If they eat it, there is the distinct possibility someone will die. They look to Elisha for the answer. He tells them to bring him some flour to add to the pot. The addition of the flour counteracts the poison in the stew. The stew is now safe to eat.

Like the sons of the prophets we too have been in circumstances described as deadly be it physical, emotional or spiritual. There appears to be no way out. Trespassing into unknown areas, analogous to the wild gourd, we do not test but presume everything is all right. When we discover we made a mistake, we do not know how to correct it.

The sons of prophets called on Elisha for help. He had the remedy. It was flour.

We have the same remedy at Elisha's disposal. Our flour can enter into any deadly situation and render it harmless. Our flour is called, 'the bread of life.' Our bread of life's name is Yeshua (Jesus). He is more powerful than the most lethal poison. Once we call on Him, He can transform our situation.

There is no benefit to merely know about Yeshua and not call on Him to deliver us or our loved ones from perilous situations. Are you facing a life and death situation?

If so, pray now for Yeshua to come into the situation and render it harmless.

Dear Father,

Everywhere I look in my life there is the potential for death. I know of no remedy to heal my problem. I have looked to many sources for aid but none are effective. Lord God, I call on You to come into my situation.

You are my bread of life. Without You I cannot live. Without Your help, I cannot get through this situation.

Just as You did for the sons of prophets I ask You do the same for me now. Change my situation from harmful to harmless.

I believe You can do all things. The way You dealt with others is an example for me. I invite You now, dear Lord Yeshua, to enter into my situation and change it.

I am thanking You in advance for the great work You are going to do.

In Yeshua's (Jesus') name I pray,

Amen

My Redeemer Lives

Job 19:25-27 ^{25}*For I know that my Redeemer lives,
And He shall stand at last on the earth;*
^{26} *And after my skin is destroyed, this I know,
That in my flesh I shall see God,*
^{27} *Whom I shall see for myself,
And my eyes shall behold, and not another.
How my heart yearns within me!*

The Lord is close to the brokenhearted. Job has lost everything, his children, his possessions and his health. His wife, a.k.a. the great encourager, tells him to curse God and die. Thankfully, he does not take her advice.

His three best friends come to 'comfort' him in his affliction. Even though their names are Zophar, Bildad and Eliphaz they could be called Mr. Fix-It 1, 2 and 3. They never really listen to him because they are too busy trying to fix him. They accuse him and abuse him. Nevertheless, Job does not succumb to their intimidation.

God's ear is close to Job's mouth as he utters heartfelt sentiments. Job is a desperate man. The superficial niceties of society fail. Satan has stripped away all exterior trappings. Now only Job's fundamental nature remains.

Job has no advocate except God. He cries out in his desolation, **"my Redeemer lives."** The word in Hebrew for redeemer is, גאל (ga al) and means avenger, deliverer, purchaser, ransomer, and redeemer. Job knows his Redeemer can do it all for him.

Job spoke these words thousands of years before the Messiah walked the earth. God spoke to Job's spirit revealing the truth that was to come. Job could not depend on anything or anyone in the natural world. He realized his only hope was in God.

Have you ever been in a situation where all platitudes and coverings are stripped away?

Have you ever been in a condition where you have no one to turn to?

Have all your friends and family turned against you?

Have you been able to turn away from the world and turn toward God?

If this describes you then pray this prayer.

Dear Father,

I, like Job, am desperate. I have nowhere to turn. None of my friends or family understands my situation. I have suffered great loss. I know it is Satan who afflicts me. I know You will turn my bleak circumstances to good. I cannot imagine how You will do it but I know since You did it for Job You will do it for me.

I pray in agreement with Job, "For I know that my Redeemer lives,
And He shall stand at last on the earth;
And after my skin is destroyed, this I know,
That in my flesh I shall see God,
Whom I shall see for myself,
And my eyes shall behold, and not another.
How my heart yearns within me!"

All Job lost was restored to him. I believe, Lord God, You will do the same for me. Thank You for being the One I can always turn to in time of trouble.

In my Redeemer's name, I pray, Amen

When You're Having A Bad Day

Job 1:20-22 *²⁰Then Job arose, tore his robe, and shaved his head; and he fell to the ground and worshiped. ²¹And he said:*

*"Naked I came from my mother's womb,
And naked shall I return there.
The LORD gave, and the LORD has taken away;
Blessed be the name of the LORD."*
²²In all this Job did not sin nor charge God with wrong.

Job was having a bad day. First, a messenger informs him the Sabeans stole all his oxen and donkeys and killed all his servants except one. Then another servant arrives and adds a fire from heaven burnt up all the sheep and servants. Subsequently, the Chaldeans stole his camels and killed all his servants. Lastly, a tornado destroys the house where all his children were feasting and they are all dead. Job was having a very bad day.

Have you ever experienced one calamity on top of another?

Job is not alone in his suffering. Everyone has experienced tragedy. No one escapes unscathed from the hardships of life. We study Job to learn how to properly deal with catastrophic circumstances.

God tells Satan Job is an exemplary man, one who reveres God and avoids evil. He does not dabble in the occult. He does not read his horoscope in the daily paper. He does not watch sexually explicit shows on TV or go to R rated movies. He does not criticize his Pastor/Rabbi to others. He does not abuse his family verbally or physically.

In fact, he is such a commendable person that Satan catches him in his crosshairs. Satan approaches God and challenges the motivation in Job's heart. Satan claims God has made life very comfortable for Job by erecting a hedge of protection around him. Satan finds it inconceivable Job could possibly continue to love and revere God if all his earthly possessions were destroyed.

God's trust in Job is complete. He allows Satan to test Job's heart. God knows Job will be strengthened by the testing and will not fail.

When Job hears the calamitous news, he tears his clothing, shaves his head and falls on his knees to worship the Lord. Tearing clothing and shaving the head is a traditional expression of grief. First Job grieves then he worships God.

In his prayer, he remembers God as the source of all his blessings. He accepts his disastrous circumstances. Most importantly, he continues to bless God. Job's behavior is a model for us to follow.

When disaster strikes this prayer might be helpful.

Avinu Malkenu, our Father our King,

I come to You in Yeshua's (Jesus') name.

Only You know and understand the depth and breadth of this terrible tragedy that has overtaken me. In spite of all, I bless You, my Creator, my Father, my King and my God. There is none like You in Heaven or on earth. You are the mighty One able to restore, renew and rebuild.

As You restored all in Job's life I ask You to do the same in mine. No matter what happens in my life I will love You with all my heart, all my soul and all my strength. Thank You for never leaving or forsaking me. Thank You for adopting me as Your child. Amen

MISTAKES

Being A Delight To God

Proverbs 3:11-12 *¹¹My son, do not despise the chastening of the LORD,*
Nor detest His correction;
¹² For whom the LORD loves He corrects,
Just as a father the son in whom he delights.

It is a foggy day. You are lost. You barely have time to stop your car before driving into a deep ravine. Perhaps you have not experienced this scenario but everyone takes wrong turns in life. At times, it leads to life threatening situations; at other times, it leads to wasted opportunities.

Because God loves us, He wants to guide us. He is our Father. We are His sons and daughters if we have opened our hearts and allowed Him to enter. As a child of God He delights in us. The Hebrew word for delight in this verse is, רָצָה (rot tsa) and means to be pleased with; to be acceptable, set affection on, approves, delights, enjoys, likes, and pardons.

Fill your name in the blank. God delights in, is pleased with, accepts, sets His affection on, approves of, enjoys, likes and pardons _____. Now read it aloud many times until it is deep in your spirit.

We find it difficult to accept the fact God loves us. Our belief is not a condition of His love. However, doubting God's love makes us an easy target for the enemy. Walking in the head and heart knowledge of God's love strengthens us against the fiery darts of the enemy.

Just as we correct our children when they are about to do something wrong, similarly God corrects us. He sees the end from the beginning. He knows when we are on a path bound for destruction. He will use every means at His disposal to stop us from hurting ourselves.

We often perceive His correction as harsh because we have limited sight and are unaware of the disaster awaiting us at the end of the road.

During times of correction, we are to remember God's unfathomable love for us. If we have teachable spirits and do not rebel against the correction then it will accomplish its purpose.

Are you experiencing a time of correction in your life?

At the same time, do you realize how much God loves you?

Then apply this scripture through prayer into your life.

Dear Father,

I call You father because I have accepted You into my heart. I know You will never leave me or forsake me no matter what I do. But I also know You desire the best for me. If You see I am headed in the wrong direction You will stop me and turn me around.

I am in a situation now where it seems as if You are not here. But I know that is a lie from the enemy. You have not left me. I do not walk by feelings. I walk by the commandments in Your word. I believe Your word is true.

I ask for a teachable spirit. Help me to forgive others who have wronged me and/or my family. Help me learn the lessons taught through this circumstance so I can move on in my life. Help me to remember how much You love me. I love You too,

In Yeshua's (Jesus') name, Amen

Being Humble Before The Lord

2 Samuel 6:14 *"Then David danced before the LORD with all his might;"*

David loved the Lord. But David's love for the Lord did not stop him from making a mistake. When David transported the Ark of the Covenant, he put it in an ox cart. When the cart was unsteady, Uzzah placed his hand on the Ark to secure it. God was angry with Uzzah for his attitude of irreverence. The Ark was God's dwelling place, not to be treated carelessly.

David was in a quandary. How was he to transport the Ark? For safekeeping, he moves it into Obed-Edom's house. While it rests there, God blesses Obed-Edom and his entire household. There is always blessing in the presence of the Lord.

David consulted the Lord and followed the instruction of Moses by having the Levites carry the Ark on poles resting on their shoulders. As they progressed, they offered sacrifices accompanied by singing and music.

David was overjoyed and began to dance before the Lord. The euphoric outpouring from David's heart led to him to whirl with all his strength. Vigorous dancing is generally not considered royal behavior. His wife, Michal, the daughter of King Saul, knew this and rebuked him for it.

She understood royal etiquette but she did not know Godly etiquette. God wants all of us. He wants us to come to Him without any false trappings. There is no reason to pretend because He already knows the truth. The way we communicate among ourselves is inappropriate in communication with God.

Putting the Ark on the oxcart was the logical way to transport it, as if it was grain or hay. However, God was furious with the casual, contemptible way they treated His dwelling place. Uzzah found that out.

Consequently, David went into prayer to seek the Lord's way of carrying it. Once everything was in the correct order, God's order, then they could proceed.

Is it also that way in our lives?

When we attempt to accomplish things for God our way we will always be met with failure. David literally stripped himself. We need to emulate his behavior by stripping ourselves of pride, self-reliance and over valuing the opinions of men.

We need to seek God's way and follow it. Oftentimes it is not the quickest, easiest or most logical. But it is the right way.

Do you want to accomplish something in your life for the glory of God? Are you willing to be like David and dance before the Lord will all your might? Are you willing to pay the price, which may be condemnation from others? Do you need God to direct you as to His ways?

If your answers are 'yes' then you might find this prayer helpful.

Dear Father,

I too, like King David, have made a mistake. I tried to do _____ (insert your own information) using the wisdom and knowledge of men. As You know, I am not meeting with success.

Please forgive me for not doing it Your way.

Please show me how I am supposed to accomplish this project.

I desire to glorify You and to be a worker in Your kingdom.

I lay aside my casual attitude in relation to Godly pursuits. I desire to humble myself before You, disregarding the cost. I will step out and speak when I feel You are impressing me. I will hold my tongue when I do not feel Your unction to speak. I desire there be less of me and more of You.

Thank You, Lord, for being the God of second, third and fourth chances.

In the name of Your Son, Yeshua, (Jesus) I pray,

Amen

Taking Responsibility

Jeremiah 31:29-30 *²⁹In those days they shall say no more:*
'The fathers have eaten sour grapes,
And the children's teeth are set on edge.'
³⁰But every one shall die for his own iniquity; every man who eats the sour grapes, his teeth shall be set on edge.

It is very hard for us to accept responsibility for our actions. It is much easier to blame someone else. Sometimes it is our parents or our spouse. At other times, it is our boss, our teacher, our rabbi/pastor, or society itself. Or, like Aaron when he made the golden calf, he blamed the fire for crafting the golden calf. "So they gave it (the gold jewelry) to me, and I cast it into the fire, and this calf came out." Exodus 32:24.

We all know Aaron was lying. We lie for different reasons:
1) It is habitual.
2) We want people to think well of us.
3) We are unable to distinguish the truth from falsehood.
4) We are unable to tell the truth.

Lying becomes habitual when the action is repeated over and over. If the lie is not confronted it becomes comfortable in the mind of the liar. After a time it becomes easier to lie then to be truthful. Even inconsequential matters can be the subject of lies. It is very difficult for the habitual liar to tell the truth. As a result, the person is untrustworthy and loses credibility with his family and friends.

Sometimes we lie because we want people to think well of us. We may suffer from a lack of self worth. We believe if we embellish the truth people like us better. At first, we exaggerate the truth. Next, we distort the truth. Finally, we abandon the truth and invent a fanciful lie. As a result, our opposite intention is realized. Instead of people thinking well of us, when we are caught lying, they think worse of us.

At other times, rose-colored glasses obscure our perception of an incident. Our objectivity flies out the window. We relate what we want to happen rather than what actually occurred. At this point, we are in total deception and are unable to distinguish truth from falsehood.

In some instances, there are no reasons why we lie. We are incapable of telling the truth. We know we have lied and yet cannot stop.

Satan is the Father of lies. God is the Father of all truth. He sends His Ruach, (Holy Spirit) to convict us of the truth. By lying whether it is spontaneous or preconceived, we are aligning ourselves with Satan. Lying is not a characteristic beneficial to us.

Often it is as difficult to break a habit of lying, as it is to break a drug addiction. The basis of lying is a lying spirit. Satan has one third of the fallen angels in heaven working for him. These fallen angels, commonly known as demons, watch families for generations. Weaknesses in families are inherited just like hair or eye color. Lying may also be a generational weakness.

Demons are familiar with a person's genealogical shortcomings and zero in to attack. Lying demons can speak into our minds with evil suggestions. We may begin with telling inconsequential lies and then progress. Once the demons are firmly entrenched, it is very difficult to make them leave purely by using our will. God's word never fails us. The demons flee at Yeshua's (Jesus') name.

Do you want to get rid of a lying spirit? Receiving God's word and applying it to your life will set you free.

Dear Father,

There are times in my life when I do not take responsibility for my actions. I blame others and lie about things. I no longer want to do this. I know this is an obstacle for me. I want to overcome this. I desire to live a pure and holy life, pleasing to You. I ask You to help me apply Your word in my life and cleanse me from a lying spirit.

Even though I know a tendency to lie may be a generational weakness in my family, I can choose not to walk in it. In the name of Yeshua (Jesus), I take the sword of the Spirit, which is the word of God and I severe every unholy alliance between me and anyone in my family five generations on each side. I put the blood of Yeshua (Jesus) on the severed ends so they will not reattach.

Regardless of the behavior of anyone in my family I am free from his/her consequences. I am responsible for my own actions. I will not blame others for my faults.

The blood of the Lamb cleanses me from the spirit of lying. From this day forth I will walk in the purity of the Ruach Ha-Kodesh (the Holy Spirit). I thank You Lord that Your word is a consuming fire that delivers me from destruction.

In Yeshua's (Jesus') name I pray, Amen

Keeping Your Focus

I Samuel 12:20-22 *²⁰Then Samuel said to the people, "Do not fear. You have done all this wickedness; yet do not turn aside from following the LORD, but serve the LORD with all your heart. ²¹And do not turn aside; for then you would go after empty things which cannot profit or deliver, for they are nothing. ²²For the LORD will not forsake His people, for His great name's sake, because it has pleased the LORD to make you His people.*

We all make mistakes. Often times we think we are on the right track but in fact, we are not even close. The Jewish people were no different. They looked around and saw all the other nations ruled by kings. Having someone to tell you where to go and what to do brings a certain amount of security.

God has chosen the Jewish people as His own special treasure and He is their king. But the people grumbled. They wanted to be like the Jones. They loudly protested their lack of kingship. Samuel was a great prophet and judge of Israel but his sons were washouts. Samuel was getting old and the people were getting impatient so they decided for themselves that they needed a king.

When Samuel took their request to the Lord, he was told to grant it and God would choose the king. God told Samuel the people were not rejecting Samuel but were rejecting Him.

After Saul was anointed king, the people had a change of heart but it was too late. Samuel says to them, **"Do not fear"**. When we make a mistake and admit it then God says the same to us. "Don't be afraid." Consequences of our error (be it large or small) begin to loom in our imagination but remember God's words. Do not let fear prevail.

God does not sweep our actions under the carpet. He acknowledges we have made wrong choices and have done incorrect actions but He does not want us to turn away from following Him. He still wants each one of us.

In fact He still wants you to serve Him **with all your heart.** God wants as much of our hearts as we can give Him. As we grow and mature our heart capacity gets bigger and bigger. God wants to be the center of the focus of our attention.

After we make a mistake it is very easy to fall into self condemnation and guilt. Or else we submerge ourselves in work or projects in order not to deal with the fact of our error. God does not want us **to go after empty things which cannot profit or deliver for they are nothing.**

God is our Father and He wants the very best for our lives. There is not one person in this world who has not made a mistake. Some mistakes are very great and hurt other people. Sometimes we deeply regret bad choices that end up as terrible mistakes. God does not want us paralyzed by fear of error. But He does want us to admit our errors and continue to follow Him.

If your focus is fuzzy and you need some clarity then pray this prayer.

Dear Father,

I have blown it big time. You know what I've done. Sometimes I can't even stand to think about it or I pretend it never happened. Father God, I ask You to forgive me. I don't want to continue on the path I've been walking. Help me Lord to change my ways, I can't do it by myself.

I want You to be number one in my heart and in my life. I dedicate the rest of my life to serving You. Teach me how I can be of service to You.

I pray for the others I have wounded. I ask You to minister to them and take care of them.

Thank You Lord, that You are the God of hope. I now have hope my life will be back on course.

In Yeshua's (Jesus') name,

Amen

Being Wounded

Should We Forgive?

2 Samuel 18:33 *³³Then the king was deeply moved, and went up to the chamber over the gate, and wept. And as he went, he said thus: "O my son Absalom—my son, my son Absalom—if only I had died in your place! O Absalom my son, my son!"*

When Absalom was born, David had great expectations. Absalom in Hebrew, אַבְשָׁלוֹם pronounced Avshalom and means Father of Peace. David looked at this beautiful baby and spoke his hopes, desires and dreams.

Absalom grew into an extremely handsome young man. He cut his thick, luxuriant hair once a year and it weighed five pounds. The scriptures describe him as being perfect from the sole of his foot to the crown of his head. The scriptures add no one in Israel was praised as much as Absalom because of his good looks.

What went wrong in his life?

- ❖ His sister was raped by his half brother.
- ❖ His father never adequately dealt with the situation.
- ❖ He killed his sister's rapist.
- ❖ After returning from exile, his father refused to see him for many years.
- ❖ He waited for years before he tried to wrest the kingdom from his father's rule.
- ❖ He chased his father into exile.

These events shaped Absalom's life. However, Absalom always had a choice. He chose to become bitter and resentful. He harbored ill feelings toward is father for many years. He patiently worked at gaining favor with the people of Israel in order to usurp his father's throne.

Forgiveness did not seem to be a word in his vocabulary. Every time he looked at Tamar, his sister, a spinster living in his home, anger and hostility toward his father was renewed. For years he nourished and encouraged negative feelings until they became his raison d'être.

His ignominious end came as he was riding in pursuit of his father to kill him; his famous hair was caught by a branch and swung him off his mule and into the air. Joab, David's commander-in-chief, killed him hanging in the air.

David's response was heart rendering. His grief was felt by all the people of Israel. Their joyous victory was smothered by David's mourning.

Not only did David forgive Absalom for trying to overthrow his kingdom and disgrace him before the whole world; he also wanted to die in Absalom's place. David was able to forgive Absalom's vile words, deeds and thoughts. Not only did he forgive but he also continued to love him.

David was a man who made mistakes as we all do. Nevertheless, he did not make one of the biggest mistakes, which is unforgiveness. There was no root of bitterness in his heart.

Is there some bitterness in your heart? Would you rather end up like Absalom or King David? God says vengeance is His, He will repay. Forgiving does not mean we admit the actions of another were right. It means we will not let another person's wrongdoing defile our lives.

If this is an area where you need God's help then pray this prayer.

Dear Father,

I have so much pain in my heart it is hard to speak to You. You know the situation. I set my will to forgive _____ (insert name). I know You will perform the healing in my heart.

I will try to no longer think about this situation or speak of it. It is in the past and I leave it in the past. If a similar situation arises, I will not be an innocent victim. I will call on You to be my champion and guide me. I do not need to fear any longer.

Wash me in the precious blood of Your Son. I desire to be cleansed from all negative thoughts and emotions. I ask You to apply Your balm of Gilead to all the places I hurt.

I receive Your healing.

In Yeshua's (Jesus') name,

Amen

Healing Deep Wounds

Isaiah 30:26 *[26]Moreover the light of the moon will be as the light of the sun,*
And the light of the sun will be sevenfold,
As the light of seven days,
In the day that the LORD binds up the bruise of His people
And heals the stroke of their wound.

The God of Abraham, Isaac and Jacob is a God of hope. No matter the circumstances, we can lift our eyes to the Lord and know He will heal us regardless of our ailment.

We live in a world offering quick solutions to complex problems. Pills are advertised on television from perking us up to putting us to sleep and every disorder in between.

Nevertheless, quick solutions give fleeting results. Sometimes the side effects from medication will invite an entirely new set of problems. We need a lasting cure with far reaching benefits.

Some of our problems are extremely complicated. An ordinary doctor, counselor or psychiatrist is incapable of healing the depth of some of our wounds.

We all have a physician who makes house calls. His name is Yeshua (Jesus). When we accept Yeshua as the promised Messiah of Israel, we allow God to heal our lives. We live in a world covered by darkness of sin. Upon the acceptance of Yeshua, the feeble light of the moon will be transformed into the brilliant light of the sun.

The light of the sun will be intensified seven times seven, seven times by seven days. The light reveals hidden things in our lives. At times, greater understanding brings greater pain.

Aching memories, which we masked from ourselves, will be revealed in this brilliant light.

Then God, our healer, will bind up all our wounds, physical, mental, spiritual and emotional. In addition, He will heal the initial memory of the source of the stroke, which caused the wounds.

To activate this promise in your life it is necessary to appropriate it and make it your own. Write it down; personalize it with your name and your complaint, read it aloud so it enters your eyes, ears, mind and heart. During difficult times, remind God of His promises to you.

God is faithful. He will perform His word in your life. Do not allow yourself to dwell on everything that is wrong. That leads you deeper into depression and discouragement. Lift your eyes to the Lord and the glorious work He promises to fulfill in your life.

He never promises to move instantly although many times unexpectedly that happens. Because God is faithful, everything He promises will eventually come to pass.

Do you need some light shed on a dark area in your life?

Do you have a wound that refuses to heal?

Do you need God's promises realized in your life?

If so then pray this prayer.

Dear Father,

I come to You depressed and forlorn. I feel so low it is as if I am six feet under. I ask You to raise me up into the light of Your presence. I need Your healing presence in my life. Only

You understand the complexity of my problems. I have tried to find answers in this world but nothing gives me lasting relief.

I come to You. I claim Your word in my life. I believe You will perform what You have promised.

I accept Your healing without doubting.

In Yeshua's (Jesus') name,

Amen

Preparing Against Heart Attacks

Proverbs 4:23 *²³Keep your heart with all diligence, For out of it spring the issues of life.*

Attacks against the heart are the number one killer among children, teenagers, young adults, adults and seniors. It does not distinguish between males or females. It is equally virulent to all. A heart attack can kill the emotional body. Sometimes it maims. It is always destructive.

The heart attack generally originates from those we love the most. They are in a position to hurt us the most. As children, often the harsh words of parents, teachers, siblings and friends can cause massive damage to the heart area. Often it takes years to undo the harm administered by those we love.

In our teenage years we are especially susceptible to attack. At this time we are struggling to carve out our own identities. The verbal cruelty of others affects us greatly during this impressionable time.

As adults we are forming marital relationships. Too often our foundation is not based on God's word but on the sinking sand values of this world. As a result we may treat our spouse without respect, admiration or love. Physical, spiritual or verbal abuse is too often characteristic of immature relationships regardless of the ages of the people involved.

As seniors we muse over our shortcomings during our early years and regret unfortunate turns our lives have taken.

God has a remedy for every heart problem. If we follow His advice we will have long, happy and pain free lives. Troubles always come but they do not need to stay with us.

Through the writings of King Solomon we are told to **keep our heart with all diligence.** The Hebrew word for keep is נָצַר (nat tsar) and means to:

1) to watch, guard, keep
   a) we watch our hearts because they are very delicate and susceptible to attack
   b) we are to guard our hearts to prevent attacks
   c) we are to keep our hearts protected

2) to preserve and guard from dangers
   a) we are to safeguard our hearts from unholy influences
   b) we are not to enter dangerous relationships which God has warned us against

3) to keep, observe, guard with fidelity
   a) we are to remain steadfast, not veering from God's path of righteousness
   b) we are to observe the commandments of God
   c) we are to be committed to keeping our hearts pure

4) keep undisclosed and a watcher
   a) we are to keep some things in our hearts undisclosed until the appropriate time
   b) we are to watch over our hearts

We do these things because out of our hearts **spring the issues of life**. The leading of our hearts controls the direction of our lives. If we are careless, we allow all types of waste matter to enter our hearts. As a result our lives become filled with garbage.

We can control and cleanse our hearts.

Dear Father,

I come to You in Yeshua's (Jesus') name. Only You know how unhappy I am. I have taken things into my heart that are unhealthy (such as codependent relationships, reading inappropriate books and magazines, watching sexually oriented TV shows and movies, listening to coarse talk shows, etc.)

I am sorry I have done these things. I realize they are wrong. Help me to leave behind these harmful habit patterns. Wash me in Your precious blood so I can be clean. Fill me anew with Your Spirit of truth. I give You permission to move in my life and change things.

Thank You for being such a great God. There is no power in Heaven or earth that can stand against You.

In Yeshua's (Jesus') name I pray,

Amen

The Treatment Of God's Anointed

I Samuel 26:10-11 *[10]David said furthermore, "As the LORD lives, the LORD shall strike him, or his day shall come to die, or he shall go out to battle and perish. [11]The LORD forbid that I should stretch out my hand against the LORD'S anointed..."*

David found himself in a precarious situation. A lunatic, who was also his father-in-law, his king and God's anointed, was chasing him all over the countryside trying to kill him. Discussion was impossible. There were only two choices – kill or be killed.

However, David perceived the world through God's eyes. He knew he was forbidden to strike God's anointed one. At this point in time, the anointing as king had already passed to David, although he was not in possession of the throne. Samuel, the prophet, had anointed him. David could have used worldly logic to justify his overthrow of Saul. None of his followers would have objected. His most trusted advisors were encouraging him to kill Saul.

But David lived by God's commandments. He knew God disciplines those He loves. He knew God could sovereignly kill Saul. Or his appointed time to die could approach. Or he could be killed on the battlefield. But he knew he was not to be the instrument of Saul's destruction. In fact he says, **"The LORD forbid that I should stretch out my hand against the LORD'S anointed..."**

There is an unhealthy desire in the body Messiah to stretch out our hands and strangle God's anointed. We find it necessary to assume God's role to judge and persecute those who are anointed to lead, preach, and pray.

Eavesdropping at a Sunday lunch gathering it is not uncommon to see they are having the pastor, priest or rabbi for lunch. Sometimes he's (or she's) the main course. Congregants criticize everything from the tie he was wearing to the number of times she sneezed.

There are legitimate concerns congregants may have regarding doctrine. Discussing the issue is the preferable manner of resolving differences. Of course, if the pastor refuses discussion there is still a choice.

If you disagree with the doctrine preached, you can leave the congregation. You can also pray for the pastor. Prayer moves mountains. Our codependent need to take responsibility for others leads to repeated splintering of the body Messiah. We are our own worst enemy. Oftentimes we kill our own wounded. On one hand, the devil is trying his hardest to destroy God's anointed. On the other hand, we carry on where the devil stopped.

If you take your grievances to the Lord instead of opening your mouth to others then much is accomplished. When your friends inquire why you have left you can explain that you disagree with the doctrine. It is not necessary to slander the pastor.

Perhaps this teaching has brought an incident to mind that needs to be brought before the throne of grace. Or perhaps you are involved in a situation right now that needs attention.

Dear Father,

You know my heart aches. Even though some time has passed, I am still very wounded by the treatment I received at _____ (you fill in the blank). Things were said to me that were untrue or grossly exaggerated. It hurts me to think about these things.

I forgive all those who maligned me. (It helps to list them by name). I forgive them with my will and I know Lord You will do the corresponding work in my heart. I ask You to guard my lips from speaking ill of them. I ask You to move in their lives and show them the truth about this situation. I ask You to judge and discipline them because You love them.

I ask You to forgive me for speaking and gossiping about Your anointed leaders. I realize I have said and done things not pleasing to You. Please forgive me. I will try to never repeat my past mistakes. Please cleanse me from my unrighteousness. I desire to grow and mature in the image of Your Son. I accept Your forgiveness and I forgive myself.

In the name of Your Son I pray,

Amen

Serving God With Joy

2 Chronicles 30:23 *²³Then the whole assembly agreed to keep the feast another seven days, and they kept it another seven days with gladness.*

Hezekiah's reign as king of Judah was marked by a resurgence of faith in the Lord. The opulent temple Solomon built was now desecrated and filled with debris. King Hezekiah summoned all the priests and Levites to clean and sanctify the temple. Once the temple was cleansed, Hezekiah ordered the priests to make offerings to the Lord. During the sacrificial offerings the congregants worshiped, the singers sang and the shofars sounded.

After the burnt offerings were consumed King Hezekiah and all who were there bowed down and worshiped the Lord. King Hezekiah commanded the Levites to sing the psalms of David and Asaph.

As soon as the temple was cleansed Hezekiah called all of Israel and Judah to observe the Passover. Due to the wickedness of past leadership, Passover had not been celebrated. Many scoffed and ridiculed Hezekiah, refusing to come. However, Judah responded favorably and the people humbled themselves. They went throughout the countryside ripping down altars to pagan gods. Then they celebrated the Passover for seven days.

However, seven days was insufficient so the entire group decided to celebrate for **another seven days with gladness**. To fully understand this attitude we examine the Hebrew word for gladness שִׂמְחָה (sim ha) and it means glee, exceeding gladness, joy, mirth, pleasure and rejoicing.

Throughout Jerusalem there had not been a celebration of this magnitude since the time of Solomon. Then the people proceeded to go throughout the countryside destroying the remaining high places of pagan worship.

Do you have a desire to see the residents of your city destroying all vestiges of worship to false religions and glorifying the Lord?

Do you want to be like the Judeans who refused to stop worshiping the Lord and extended Passover for another seven days?

Do you want God's zeal to fill your heart and entire being?

If so then you need to follow Hezekiah's example:

- ❖ Cleanse your temple
    - Work on changing negative thought processes
    - Stop giving the devil the control of your tongue
    - Focus on the Lord and not yourself
- ❖ Make an offering to the Lord
    - Give a needy person an anonymous gift
    - Go out of your way to physically help someone
    - Be kind to an unkind person
- ❖ Worship the Lord with music and psalms
    - Put on a praise CD and sing along with it
    - Read some psalms out loud
    - Make up your own song and sing it to the Lord
- ❖ Celebrate God's holy days whole-heartedly
    - Observe God's rules for the Sabbath
    - Do not let your Sabbath experience stop when you leave your congregation
    - Search the scriptures to learn the significance of the Lord's feasts
- ❖ Worship God with joy

The only way to change your city is to change yourself. Decide today if you want to see God's glory in your life, in your city and in your country. You can make a difference.

Dear Father,

I want to change my life. Help me to get rid of years of worthless trash accumulating in my heart and mind. I no longer want to carry unforgiveness, hatred, bitterness, dislike, mockery, and hardness. I release these things to You.

Fill my heart with Your love for others. Help me to set aside my self absorption and shyness in order to reach out to others.

Fill my mind with Your songs, psalms and word.

Fill my life with Your overflowing joy. Help me to touch others with Your joy.

In Yeshua's (Jesus') name I pray,

Amen

DELIVERANCE

Living In The Shadow Of Death

Isaiah 9:2 *²The people who walked in darkness*
Have seen a great light;
Those who dwelt in the land of the shadow of death,
Upon them a light has shined.

We live in **the shadow of death**. Every person on this earth will die. Death awaits us from the moment we are born. Our natural state, in this world, is one of darkness. We grope our way from one day to the next hoping to reach islands of security. The path is not illuminated or the way clear. There are hindrances and obstacles every direction we turn. Since our passageway is darkened, we often collide with hidden objects. This is the situation of unregenerate man.

When you are in a state of darkness, even a small light seems bright. In our darkness, God gave us a bright light and His name is Yeshua (Jesus) which in Hebrew means salvation. Through the saving power of accepting Yeshua (Jesus) in our hearts darkness is transformed into light. The power of God's salvation takes us out of the land of the shadow of death and moves us into the land of eternal life.

Our efforts do not cause this. The scripture says, **"Upon them a light has shined."** God's mercy not our labors bring our deliverance. We no longer need to stumble in darkness. **A great light** is available to us.

However, we have a choice. We can open our eyes and accept the illumination of the light or we can shut our eyes tightly denying the light exists. No one can force us to open our eyes. We can even open them for a second and tightly shut them again. Or we can say we do not need the light. Only weak people need the light. We can manage the darkness by ourselves.

God shines His light in the form of His Son Yeshua (Jesus) upon us. He does not take His light away. He does not force us to accept the light. He waits for us to freely open our eyes.

Have you ever opened your eyes to God's light, His Son Yeshua (Jesus)?

Are you tired of bumping into obstacles as you grope your way around?

Are you willing to allow God to show you His Son?

Do you want the assurance of knowing that after you leave this earth you will live forever with the Lord?

If your answers to the previous questions are 'yes' then pray this prayer.

Dear Father in Heaven and on earth,

I am tired of walking in darkness. I have tried doing things my way and they have not worked out very well. I am willing to open my eyes and accept the atoning death of Yeshua on the tree. I accept the fact that by His death my sins are washed away.

While stumbling in the darkness I have done some things that are wrong and I have hurt some people. I ask You to forgive me for all the bad things I have done to others and to myself. Please shine Your light on those I have wronged. I know through the light of Your word and Your presence my life can change. Do likewise with others I have adversely affected. I willingly accept that change in my life. In fact, I welcome it.

Teach me how to walk correctly through life. Show me the proper path to follow so I do not fall and hurt others and myself.

Thank You for loving me so much that You sent Your light, Your Son, to teach me how to live and not die.

In Yeshua's (Jesus') name I pray,

Amen

We Are Never Forsaken Or Forgotten

Isaiah 49:14-18 ¹⁴*But Zion said, "The LORD has forsaken me,*
And my Lord has forgotten me."
¹⁵ *"Can a woman forget her nursing child,*
And not have compassion on the son of her womb?
Surely they may forget,
Yet I will not forget you.
¹⁶ *See, I have inscribed you on the palms of My hands;*
Your walls are continually before Me.
¹⁷ *Your sons shall make haste;*
Your destroyers and those who laid you waste
Shall go away from you.
¹⁸ *Lift up your eyes, look around and see;*
All these gather together and come to you.
As I live," says the LORD,
"You shall surely clothe yourselves with them all as an ornament,
And bind them on you as a bride does.

The Jewish people, looking at their circumstances, had excellent reasons to believe God had forsaken and forgotten them. They were ripped away from their homes, transported to foreign lands, and lost everything except their belief in the God of Abraham, Isaac and Jacob.

We too, at times, seemingly have excellent reasons to believe God has forsaken and forgotten us. We look at circumstances and become depressed. Our eyes stare into the wrong places. We are to be fixing our focus, at all times, on the Lord.

He tells us why we are not to feel forsaken or forgotten.

- ❖ It is impossible for a nursing mother to **forget her nursing child**. Her body gives her a very strong physical reminder that it is chow time. God is telling us His tie to us is so strong it is as if His body aches if He forgets us.

- ❖ God always goes the extra mile. He says even if a woman should forget her nursing child His attachment to us is so much more compassionate that He would never forget us.

- ❖ There are certain lines on our palms. No amount of scrubbing will erase them. We are those lines on God's palms. He says, **"See, I have inscribed you on the palms of My hands."** We are part of Him. He would have to forget Himself to forget us.

- ❖ Our **walls are continually before Him**. In biblical times, walls enclosed and defined the size of the city. God is saying the sum total of all we are is continually before Him. Not one iota of our being is excluded.

- ❖ God will cause all our enemies to leave us. Enemies can be either people and/or spirits. Evil spirits of infirmity, depression, anger, etc. are included in this promise.

- ❖ God orders us to lift our eyes from our circumstances and look up. He is not only going to defeat our enemies but also make them into a piece of jewelry we can wear to remind us of His victory for us.

Israel is in the midst of horrific times. Innocent men, women and children are targets for the enemy. God's promises to Israel never became void. He will accomplish all He has promised her.

This should be a great assurance for us. God is faithful. He will deliver us as well as the Jewish people and the state of Israel.

Dear Father,

Forgive me for doubting Your power to deliver. I refuse to let my eyes constantly dwell on my problems. I lift my eyes to You. I claim Your promises in my life. I believe You will never leave me or forsake me.

After hundreds of years of wandering by the Jewish people You brought them back to their land. You can do the same for my life. I trust You.

I thank You for all You have done and will do for me and my family.

In Yeshua's (Jesus') name I pray,

Amen

Turning Sorrow To Joy

Esther 9:20-22 *[20] And Mordecai wrote these things and sent letters to all the Jews, near and far, who were in all the provinces of King Ahasuerus, [21] to establish among them that they should celebrate yearly the fourteenth and fifteenth days of the month of Adar, [22] as the days on which the Jews had rest from their enemies, as the month which was turned from sorrow to joy for them, and from mourning to a holiday; that they should make them days of feasting and joy, of sending presents to one another and gifts to the poor.*

Anti-Semitism is not an invention of the twentieth century. In the time of Nehemiah and Ezra anti-Semitism was alive and well in Persia. King Ahasuerus, ruler of Persia, deposes his wife, Queen Vashti, and after a lengthy search decides on Hadassah, a beautiful, young, Jewish girl, to be her successor. However, under the wise tutelage of her uncle, Mordecai, she uses the Persian name Esther, and hides her Jewish identity.

Haman, close advisor to the king, rages against Mordecai, who in strict observance of the Law of Moses will not bow down to him. Haman hatches a plot to kill not only Mordecai but also all the Jewish people living under the rule of King Ahasuerus. The King without a second thought easily allows the massacre to take place on a date determined by casting Pur (lots).

Esther intervenes on behalf of her people, reveals her Jewish identity to the King and stops the massacre. Haman is hanged and Mordecai assumes a position of leadership second to King Ahasuerus.

To this day Jews continue to commemorate the event with the celebration of Purim. The name comes from the casting of the Pur (lots), which God changed from a day of annihilation to a day of liberation. God took a hopeless situation offering death and destruction and turned it into a time of rejoicing and celebration.

In modern times, Jewish people celebrate Purim by dressing in costumes and retelling the story of Esther in humorous ways. During the retelling of the Purim story, everyone receives a grogger (noisemaker). At the mention of the name of Haman, everyone spins their groggers, stamps their feet and loudly boos. Traditionally, hamantaschen, a triangular shaped pastry filled with fruit, is eaten. The triangular shape symbolizes Haman's hat. Baskets of food are prepared and delivered to less fortunate people so they too can share in the celebration of God's deliverance of His Jewish people.

Have you ever experienced God's deliverance in your life?

Have you told this experience to your children and friends?

Have you taken time to celebrate God's acting on your behalf in a difficult circumstance?

Would you like to thank God?

Dear Father,

Thank You so much for turning a time of sorrow into joy. I desire to celebrate Your goodness in my life by sharing and witnessing to others. I realize I can rejoice in You.

There are some sorrowful areas in my life but I hand these to You and know You can turn these into joy. I thank You in advance for the great things You will do in my life.

In Yeshua's (Jesus') name, Amen

Being Seen By God

2 Chronicles 3:1 *¹Now Solomon began to build the house of the LORD at Jerusalem on Mount Moriah, where the LORD had appeared to his father David, at the place that David had prepared on the threshing floor of Ornan the Jebusite.*

The Lord entrusted Solomon to build a house for Him even though King David originally requested to build it. God explained to David that he was unqualified because he was a man of war. Solomon's name in Hebrew is שלמֹה (Shlomo) and means peaceful.

The site Solomon selected was Mount Moriah. Solomon, who had the gift of wisdom, placed the temple of God on a mountain whose name translated in English, is "being seen by God." Solomon wanted the temple to be in a location easily accessible to God.

The specific place appointed for the erection of the temple is the threshing floor of Ornan the Jebusite. In the time of King David, a terrible plague swept through the land of Israel. God stationed an angel, standing with drawn sword over Jerusalem, by the threshing floor.

After purchasing the threshing floor, David erected an altar to the Lord. There he sacrificed. At that point, the Lord had the angel replace his sword in his sheath. Jerusalem and Israel were spared.

God's eyes were on Abraham when he offered up Isaac as a sacrifice. Again Mount Moriah, mentioned in Genesis 22:2, is the place where God sees Abraham's faithfulness. He sends an angel to stop Abraham from killing Isaac and provides a substitute sacrifice, a ram, to take Isaac's place.

Do we want to be seen by God under all circumstances? We all want God to notice us when we have helped others or been especially kind in a difficult situation. What about when we lose patience with our spouse or are rude to the telemarketer? Do we want to be seen by God when we are not lovely or lovable?

At all times, we carry our temples with us and are seen by God. Just as Solomon offered sacrifices in the temple, we offer sacrifices through the way we live our lives. When we answer a harsh word with gentleness, we are offering God the sacrifice of our anger. We present our anger to Him.

When Murphy's Law is active in our lives and everything that can go wrong does go wrong we can offer our difficulties to God. Instead of being depressed and hopeless, we can praise God, thanking Him that tomorrow will be better. We demonstrate faith believing He will not let circumstances remain the same. We present our burdens as burnt offerings knowing the aroma is pleasing to Him.

Are there some areas in your life you would like to sacrifice to the Lord?

Dear Father,

I come into Your throne room and offer before You the sacrifice of my anger. In dealing with difficult people at work and at home, I will try to lay aside my natural anger and respond in a kind and loving way.

There are other areas in my life where You and I know I need help. I give You permission to work in these areas. Help me to change my behavior. I want my life to be an acceptable offering to You. Show me what needs to be changed. Through the love of Your Son, Yeshua (Jesus), I pray, Amen

Do Not Sorrow – Rejoice!

Nehemiah 8:9-10 *⁹And Nehemiah, who was the governor, Ezra the priest and scribe, and the Levites who taught the people said to all the people, "This day is holy to the LORD your God; do not mourn nor weep." For all the people wept, when they heard the words of the Law.*

¹⁰Then he said to them, "Go your way, eat the fat, drink the sweet, and send portions to those for whom nothing is prepared; for this day is holy to our Lord. Do not sorrow, for the joy of the LORD is your strength."

Nehemiah and Ezra are contemporaries having returned from the Babylonian captivity by order of King Cyrus and later King Darius of Persia (Persia had conquered Babylon.) They are equally instrumental in rebuilding the temple in Jerusalem and restoring the Jewish people to their land.

After much opposition, the temple and walls around the city are rebuilt. Ezra, the priest, calls the people together and proceeds to read the Book of the Law of Moses.

The people's reaction is astonishing. Great weeping sweeps through the crowd to such an extent that Ezra directs them not to sorrow but to rejoice in the Lord. After seventy years of living in a foreign land under foreign gods, they are finally in their homeland under the God of Abraham, Isaac and Jacob.

Great emotion fills their hearts. The neighboring inhabitants and enemies of God did not want Jerusalem and the temple rebuilt. Through trickery and lies, every attempt is made to discourage and halt the ongoing work. Nevertheless, God, as always, prevails.

As a culmination of the building project, Ezra the priest reads the Book of the Law of Moses. The presence of the Lord is so powerful that the people can only weep. However, God does not desire their sorrow. Through Ezra He tells them to return to their business, celebrate by eating the fat (considered a delicacy) and sharing with others who have less. He declares this day holy to the Lord and tells them by being joyful in God will they derive their strength.

That principle still holds true today. In the midst of great hardship, we must remember God has not forgotten us. Deliverance will come at the appointed time. Following deliverance is restoration. The joy of our restoration is to be shared with others less fortunate than ourselves.

Have you experienced great sorrow? Has God delivered you?

Have you encouraged others still caught in the morass of hardship?

Do you want to be a blessing to God and to others? If so then pray this prayer.

Dear Lord,

Even though You have brought me out of the pit I still have very little joy. It seems part of me is dead. I ask You to revive my 'rejoicer'. I know that joy in You is my strength but I have very little strength.

Build me up in You. Give me a grateful heart. Help me to stop reliving the past. I believe old things do pass away and all things become new. Help me to share my new found joy with others. Thank You for being a God who enjoys the joy of His children. May these things come to pass in my life,

In Yeshua's (Jesus') name I pray, Amen

OBEDIENCE

Doing The Right Thing

Jeremiah 20:9 *⁹Then I said, "I will not make mention of Him, Nor speak anymore in His name."
But His word was in my heart like a burning fire
Shut up in my bones;
I was weary of holding it back,
And I could not.*

Has doing the right thing ever gotten you into trouble?

The prophet Jeremiah was an expert on speaking forth on politically incorrect topics. He was not Mr. Popularity. He faithfully and passionately presented God's pronouncements concerning His people.

Did everyone applaud after Jeremiah spoke? Did they pat him on the back and say, "Praise God that was an anointed word brother"? Did they listen to his words and try to apply them?

The answer to all the questions above is 'no'.

Jeremiah was not the bearer of good news. He gave unpopular messages straight from the Spirit of God. However, Jeremiah being a man, at times sought a lower profile. He tried to stifle God's edicts. However, he could not. He says, **"His word was in my heart like a burning fire shut up in my bones."**

Have you ever sensed God's word so vividly inside yourself?

God chose Jeremiah for His service. Has God chosen you? If you are a believer then the answer is 'yes'. The extent of service depends on your willingness to be obedient. God's calling does not always win friends and influence people. Speaking God's word will often generate many attacks against you.

Friends and family members often stoke the furnace of affliction. Has the fire singed your eyebrows as it blew up in your face? Have you, like Jeremiah, tried to withdraw?

After a time you too will be unable to hold back from serving God. You will be forced to decide whether you serve God or serve man. Once you have served God, it is difficult to stop. It becomes far more painful to stop serving God than to serve Him.

Speaking on politically incorrect topics at your children's school, at your workplace or even at your congregation is not easy or pleasant. We are living at a time when the demarcation between believers and non-believers is becoming more pronounced. Whose camp will you join?

A few guidelines may make your choice easier.

1) Make sure you are definitely hearing from the Lord and not promoting your own agenda
2) Pray before you approach anyone
3) Ask the Lord to give you the proper words at the proper time
4) Follow the correct order seeking the appropriate people to contact
5) Make sure there is less of you and more of Him
6) Forgive others if you as the servant of the Lord are not received well
7) Release everything to the Lord

Dear Holy Father,

I desire to serve You. I ask You to work and to will for Your purposes in my life. You know my strengths and my weaknesses. I ask You to use me for Your glory.

Protect me from the slings and arrows of those around me. Help me to walk in Your truth. I bind all lying and deceiving spirits trying to pull me off course. Keep me under the shadow of Your wings.

In Yeshua's (Jesus') name I pray,

Amen

Doing Things God's Way

Judges 7:2 ²*"And the LORD said to Gideon, "The people who are with you are too many for Me to give the Midianites into their hands, lest Israel claim glory for itself against Me, saying, 'My own hand has saved me.'*

There is one problem with being capable. We tend to rely on ourselves. We have accomplished tasks in life and achieved milestones. In the eyes of the world, this is a good thing. In God's eyes, it makes us a liability.

We tend to push God's ways aside and rely upon old tried and true methods. We do not wait to hear God's approach but very often, try our way first. Only after we meet with disappointment and/or defeat will we take the time to seek out God's method.

Like Gideon, we often set off in the correct direction but then go astray.

1. **We have to be clear on what we are to accomplish.**
   The Angel of the Lord appears before Gideon and tells him it is his job to wipe out the Midianites. After testing God three times, Gideon finally believes he is to be the redeemer of Israel against the Midianites.

2. **We set aside time to pray before we embark upon a course of action.**
   In his zeal, Gideon gathered thirty two thousand men to attack the Midianites. In Gideon's mind, the Midianites were a formidable foe. They destroyed the Israelites harvests and harshly oppressed them for seven years. Gideon knew

God's aim but did not consult Him as to His method. As a result, the many months Gideon spent gathering his army was time wasted while the oppressive conditions continued.

3. **Why is God's way better?**
God corrects us when we are off course. God determines victory or defeat. He withholds victory from the Israelites when they are so numerous because they would become self-reliant and forget Him. It is not until Gideon's army is whittled down to three hundred; one percent of his original army, then God allows him to fight the Midianites.

4. **Why does it bother God if we do it our way?**
Will we, like the Israelites, be tempted to say, **"My own hand has saved me"**? Yes, that is human nature. God wants us following Him and giving Him the glory.

5. **Is it easy to follow God?**
It was not easy for Gideon. Before he began his mission, he asked for three confirmations:
- The meal be consumed by fire
- The fleece should be wet but the ground dry
- The fleece should be dry but the ground wet

Seeing three miracles performed before his eyes gave him courage to believe God's instruction. He proceeded to gather his army. However, it was 'his' army, not the Lord's.

After his army becomes the Lord's army, he still hesitates to attack. One night God has Gideon and his servant, Purah, sneak into the Midian camp. They overhear a soldier telling his dream concerning Gideon's defeating the Midianites. At this point Gideon truly believes the Lord and launches the attack to gain God's victory.

Are you meeting defeat every way you turn? Perhaps it is time to try God's way.

Dear Father,

I am tired of doing it my way. Help me to seek and discover Your way. Forgive me for not putting You first but exalting the ways of the world above Your ways. Teach me how to gain victory through You. Show me Your plan and purpose for my life.

Thank You Lord for being patient with me, for knowing my shortcomings and frailties and forgiving them. Grow and mature me into the person You want me to be.

I pray all these things in the name that is above every name, the name of Your precious Son, Yeshua (Jesus).

Amen

Following Instructions
(For Ruth Adler, a wise, loving and listening spiritual mother)

Proverbs 1:8-9 *[8]My son, hear the instruction of your father, And do not forsake the law of your mother; [9]For they will be a graceful ornament on your head, And chains about your neck.*

It is impossible to live a successful life without following instructions. King Solomon wrote Proverbs to teach methods of victorious living. Role models are shapers and molders of our lives. When we look at our fathers and mothers, oftentimes our vision is obscured by their faults.

Their flaws leap to the foreground and obstruct the rest of the picture. Whether we like it or not, our parents have a major influence on who we are. We can spend a lifetime rebelling against the treatment from our parents or we can choose to forgive. We cannot change them but we can change our reactions and ourselves.

Once we forgive them, we can see characteristics and behaviors in us that are inherited from them. All parents want their children to be successful. However, all parents are not effective parents and may have never learned how to raise children with wisdom and tolerance. This does not negate the fact that on some level they wish their children to do well.

A father or mother can be natural, adopted or spiritual. If we are wise, we will follow their instructions. Solomon advises us to **hear**. The Hebrew word is שָׁמַע (sha ma) and means to hear intelligently, attentively, carefully, to consider, discern, listen, obey, perceive, regard, and understand.

We are to hear the **instruction** מוּסָר (mu sar) of our father figure. Instructions are not the blueprint we follow to put a bicycle together. The word means chastisement, reproof, warning, instruction, restraint, chastening, correction, discipline, and rebuke. These are not nice things or things we like to hear. Yet if we desire wisdom, they are to be carefully considered.

Our mothers say other things to us. We are warned not to **forsake** נָטַשׁ (na tash) the laws of our mothers. The word in Hebrew means thrust off, reject, cast off, let fall, and forsake.

If we follow the wise instructions of our father and mother, we receive a promise from God. Our obedience will adorn us greater than gold and jewels. We will wear **a graceful ornament** or a wreath of grace, חֵן (hen) on our heads. Grace in this context means graciousness, kindness, favor, beauty on our heads and as a necklace on our necks.

Would you like to wear this kind of jewelry?

If this is a difficult area for you then pray this prayer.

Dear Father,

I have a hard time hearing anything from my parents. Please help me to forgive them. I forgive them with my will and I ask You to do the work in my heart.

Help me sift out the advice they have given me that is valuable and worthwhile. Help me to honor them and speak well of them. I desire graciousness, kindness and favor to rest on my head and around my neck. Continue to teach me to move in wisdom in all areas of my life.

In Yeshua's (Jesus') name I pray, Amen

The Importance Of Finishing

2 Kings 13:18-19 *¹⁸Then he said, "Take the arrows"; so he took them. And he said to the king of Israel, "Strike the ground"; so he struck three times, and stopped. ¹⁹And the man of God was angry with him, and said, "You should have struck five or six times; then you would have struck Syria till you had destroyed it! But now you will strike Syria only three times."*

Israel was in desperate straits. Their enemy the Syrians cruelly oppressed them. There was no expectation of release from their hand. Joash, king of Israel, approaches Elisha seeking wisdom and deliverance for his people.

Even though Elisha is dying from a terminal illness, he still counsels King Joash. Elisha always gave God his best regardless of his personal condition. He knew King Joash was seeking a word from the Lord on behalf of God's people, Israel. Elisha did not say, "Come back later when I feel better." or, "It's not convenient for me to talk to you right now." Elisha took care of God's business, which became his business.

King Joash, on the other hand, was a relatively good king with failings. When told by Elisha to strike the ground he only struck it three times. The Hebrew word for strike is נָכָה (na kah) and it means to either strike lightly or severely. King Joash understood the instructions; however, he used his own judgment in the application. Consistent with prior behavior in not removing the pagan places of worship in Israel, he also did not complete Elisha's directions fully.

Elisha was distraught. Because of King Joash's half-hearted actions, Syria would only be briefly defeated. However, after a time she would regroup and again be a formidable foe against Israel.

Whose life does your life resemble, King Joash's or Elisha's? Do you always give every job your best effort? Do you desire, in all you do to be pleasing to the Lord? If this is an area where you need some improvement then pray this prayer.

Dear Father,

I remember times in my life when I have not completely done what I should have. Consequently, the result was not what I had hoped. I know there is nothing I can do about this now. But I do not want to continue to be the type of person who does a job halfway.

I ask You Lord to change me. I am incapable of changing myself. I need Your help. I ask You to place a desire in my heart to always do my best regardless of personal circumstances.

But at the same time, Lord, I ask You to free me from a self centered desire for perfection. No one on this earth is perfect and I am no exception. Help me not to be caught up in self-striving and self-condemnation.

I know You forgive me for all I did in the past that was not whole hearted. I receive Your forgiveness. I look forward to serving You and others with a whole heart and a good attitude. I will try to finish every task in a timely manner and to the best of my ability.

Thank You Lord for being a great God capable of doing miracles in my heart and changing my life.

In the name of Your Son, Yeshua (Jesus), I pray,

Amen

TRUSTING GOD

Under God's Eyes

2 Chronicles 16:9 *⁹For the eyes of the LORD run to and fro throughout the whole earth, to show Himself strong on behalf of those whose heart is loyal to Him.*

At the same time, it is a comforting yet terrifying thought that the eyes of God are constantly upon us. It is all right if He sees us at services, or visiting our friends, or succeeding at work. However, He also sees us when we are angry, sad, depressed, lonely and joyless.

His eyes never stop running; they never blink; they miss nothing. The verb, run, is in the present tense and implies continuous action. We are under constant scrutiny by God.

Is this a good place?

The resounding answer is YES because:

- ❖ He shows Himself strong on our behalf
    - God is not conditional. He does not expect us to perfect ourselves. He does not set goals for us to reach. He does not keep a tally of how well we perform.
    - We are allowed to be weak, to fail, to misunderstand, and to be inadequate. It does not depend on us but on Him. His strength is perfect in our weakness.
- ❖ We are never alone.
    - We may be in a dark situation that seems as if we are utterly alone. We are not because we believe God. He tells us His eyes are constantly on us.

- When attempting a new venture sometimes it seems as if we only have ourselves to rely on. That is not true. God's eyes have not left us.

Is there anything we have to do to be constantly under God's gaze?

Our heart has to be loyal to Him. The Hebrew word for loyal is שָׁלֵם (sha lem) and means complete, friendly, full, just, made ready, peaceable, perfect quiet, whole. God wants all of our heart. He does not want shared affection. If we place God above all else in our lives then He promises to be strong on our behalf.

He is not a halfway God. In the long run, He will never disappoint us, break His promises or deceive us. He asks for a commitment of our affections to Him. He does not ask for our bank account, our time or our families. He asks for our heart. Once we love Him as much as we can then we decide how we want to share our bank account, our time and our families with Him.

Is it so hard to give your heart to God?

Have you given Him only a part and are still holding some back?

Do you want to enter a deeper relationship with God?

If so then pray this prayer.

Dear Father,

I thank You that Your eyes are always on me. I am not ashamed and do not want to hide anything from You. I know You love me as I am. All You ask is for my heart. You know my heart has been badly wounded. It is very hard to love anyone. But I make the commitment to love You.

*I love You with all my heart. I believe You will be strong on my behalf, specifically in the situation involving _____.
I receive and will depend on Your constant strength that never wavers.*

Teach me how to love You more.

In the name of Your Son I pray,

Amen

Making Up Your Mind

I Kings 18:21 *²¹And Elijah came to all the people, and said, "How long will you falter between two opinions? If the LORD is God, follow Him; but if Baal, follow him." But the people answered him not a word.*

Do you find it hard to make and then stay with a decision?

Are you often torn between several alternatives?

Do you doubt your ability to make the right decision?

If you answered yes to the previous questions then you are not alone. The nation of Israel, in the time of Elijah, had a weighty decision on her mind. The people were under the rule of the evil king Ahab. He encouraged the worship of the Baal and tried to turn the peoples' hearts against the Lord.

God raised up the powerful prophet, Elijah, to speak the truth to His people. He prepared a challenge between the powers of God Almighty versus Baal. No surprise, God won.

What about your life? Whom do you follow?

We no longer have Baal to follow but other beliefs have taken his place. Worship of self has grown in popularity. How many of us have placed ourselves on the throne. Our every want and desire is answered instantly; never to be denied.

Do you worship sports? Would you miss going to services in order to see the playoff or would you listen with an ear bug as your body sat in the pew?

Do you worship your children? Do they take precedence over everything, including God, in your life?

In the scripture, the Hebrew word for falter is פָּסַח (pa sah) and literally means to hop. Do you find yourself hopping between two ideas, unable to make up your mind?

Is there an issue in your life where you are unsure that God is who He says He is? Until you are walking in the confidence of trusting in God, you will not achieve peace.

The following is a suggested remedy for your situation.
  a) Honestly tell the Lord your doubts, fears and worries.
  b) Ask the Lord for a scripture verse or illustration that relates to your issue. You might use a concordance for assistance.
  c) Pray your verse to the Lord, seeking His guidance and clarification of your problem.
  d) Write down your scripture verse and corresponding answer. Periodically review your questions and God's answers in order to build your faith.
  e) Thank Yeshua (Jesus) for intervening, on your behalf, before the throne of grace.

Dear Father,

No one knows me better than You do. You know the difficulty I have making decisions. Very often I fear I will make a mistake. Instead of choosing the wrong thing I just do nothing.

I know this is not the way You want me to be. I trust You to guide me as I make decisions. I come against the fear of wrong decisions in the name of Yeshua (Jesus). I will use Your word as a handbook for making decisions.

In Yeshua's (Jesus') name I pray, Amen

For This Child I Have Prayed

I Samuel 1:27-28 *²⁷For this child I prayed, and the LORD has granted me my petition which I asked of Him. ²⁸Therefore I also have lent him to the LORD; as long as he lives he shall be lent to the LORD."*

How many of us have problems with our children? Our children are our legacy. We do our best to nourish and educate them emotionally, physically and spiritually. We invest our time, money and life force into them.

But what goes wrong? When we have done our best why are there so many problems?

Perhaps it is because we have neglected a fundamental truth which Hannah, the mother of Samuel, was able to grasp. Hannah has a hard time getting pregnant. She fervently prays for the Lord to give her a child. God answers and gives her a son, Samuel שְׁמוּאֵל (Sh mu el) which means God Heard. Hannah knows to whom this child belongs – he belongs to God. Therefore, after he is weaned she 'lends' him to God for service in the Temple under Eli the Priest.

Under Hannah's circumstances, would we have done this? It seems doubtful. It is human nature to cling ever tightly to people we hold precious. However, Hannah had a much better comprehension of God's ways.

By following God's plan, many wonderful events were able to take place:
1. Hannah who was formerly barren became fertile
2. Hannah had a son named Samuel

3. Hannah was blessed with more children
4. Samuel, her son, became a great prophet
5. All of Israel profited having Samuel as their spiritual leader

What can we learn from Hannah's example?
1. We need to realize our children belong to the Lord.
2. We cannot control our children.
3. We are to teach our children from our own example.
4. We are to pray constantly for our children.
5. We are to claim God's promises for their lives.
6. We are to seek God's wisdom to instruct us on how to parent correctly.
7. We are to trust God and stop worrying.

Hannah's harsh treatment by her husband's other wife, Peninnah, helped her realize her son belonged to the Lord. She did not know if she would have any other children, nonetheless, she released her only child into the service of the Lord. She did not try to control him.

Her Godly example helped mold and shape Samuel into a great leader. Even though Hannah did not live with Samuel, it does not mean she forgot about him. Every year she brought him a handmade robe. All year, as she made the little robe, it is likely she spoke her hopes and aspirations for him to God.

She claimed the best for his life. She sought God's instruction on how to parent correctly. Her firm belief in God banished her worries. Living with Eli and his corrupt sons was not the ideal situation for a young boy but through Hannah's persevering prayers Samuel was untouched by the ungodliness of Eli's sons.

None of our situations is the same but all can benefit by taking them to the Lord.

Dear Father,

You know the heaviness in my heart. You know all about the problems with my son/daughter _____ (enter the name here). You understand the situation much better than I do.

I release all control of my child over to You. Help me to be a Godly example for my child. Impress me with areas needing improvement. I give You permission to enter these areas in my life and change me. As I read Your word I ask You to quicken promises to me for my child. I will write these promises down and try to pray them daily. Please show me how to be the most effective parent for my child.

I give You all my cares and concerns. I will not intentionally worry. I will glory in Your presence and in the presence of Your Son. I will love You always.

In Yeshua's (Jesus') name,

Amen

The Faithfulness Of God

Deuteronomy 7:9 *⁹Therefore know that the LORD your God, He is God, the faithful God who keeps covenant and mercy for a thousand generations with those who love Him and keep His commandments;*

To believe your prayers will be answered you need to believe in the answerer. Who is your God?

First, **He is God**. He is the real McCoy accept no substitutes. He is not Allah and He is not Mohammed. He is God. He is not your pastor, priest or rabbi. All men have faults. None is perfect except God. He is not your father, mother or friend. He is not a man that He should lie. He is not your bank account, your house or the stock market. You cannot love God and money.

Secondly, He is **the faithful God**. Faithfulness means He is someone you can trust. Faithfulness means He will never let you down. Faithfulness does not mean that He will always do it your way. His ways are far above ours. Nevertheless, you can trust His ways. Try not to always look at the immediate circumstances. Sometimes God is molding and shaping us and those we love to become what we desire to be. The molding and shaping process is not always pleasant. We are accustomed and familiar with our old selves. However, you can teach an old dog new tricks as long as God is the teacher.

Thirdly, He **keeps covenant**. His covenant is His contract with us. God is a lawful God. He makes a contract with us and He is the only one who signs it. His contract with us is unbreakable. No high priced lawyer can find a loophole. His covenant insures our safety. Regardless of adverse circumstances, He will stay true to His covenant.

Fourthly, He shows us **mercy**. He does not punish us as we deserve rather He always extends His mercy toward us. He looks at us with kind compassion. As long as we ask for forgiveness, He will forgive us. Only He can understand our harsh trials and tribulations. His mercy endures forever.

Fifthly, His covenant and mercy endure for a **thousand generations**. A thousand generations is approximately 70,000 years. That is a very long time. That means His covenant and mercy will extend to your children, your grandchildren, your great grandchildren, your great great grandchildren, your great great great grandchildren and on and on for longer than we can imagine.

Sixthly, this promise is for a specific audience – **those who love Him.** This love thing is very important to God. Heart love deepens as time goes on. The way we love Him today is greater than the way we loved Him last year and yet is less than the way we will love Him next year.

This promise is also for those who **keep His commandments**. We are told in the Brit HaDasha (the New Covenant) all the commandments can be distilled into two: love your neighbor as yourself and love the Lord with all your heart, all your mind and all your strength. Love is progressive. It deepens and grows. Even if you do not consider yourself a loving person, you can ask God to teach you.

If you need some heart stretching, perhaps because your heart is breaking, then pray the following prayer.

Dear Father,

Help me to trust You. I need You to help me. I believe You are faithful not only to me but to all my family even for generations to come. Teach me how to be a more loving person toward You, my family, my friends, my boss, my coworkers and all I come in contact with. I desire to grow and change for the better. I ask You to be the molder and shaper of my life.

In the name of Your son, Yeshua (Jesus), I pray,

Amen

Loss Of A Loved One

Joshua 23:14 *¹⁴"I am going the way of all the earth."*

I am going the way of all the earth is a phrase used by Joshua as he tells his people he is going to die. It seems very natural. In the autumn the leaves fall to the earth; the grass starts to turn brown; the flowers lose their blooms. There is 'death' all around us. However, do we perceive it that way? Autumn is the time to rake leaves, drink hot apple cider and make the first fire in the fireplace. It is the celebration of the end of a life cycle.

If death seems to be such a natural occurrence then why do we fear it? Death is the time **to go the way of ALL the earth.** There are no exceptions. If there is a time for birth then there is a time for death.

Joshua was one hundred and ten when it was his time to **go the way of all the earth**. He continued the work of Moses and accomplished all the Lord had asked of him.

Those of us who believe in Messiah Yeshua have the assurance of continuance of life even after physical death. Our spirits will live on. The essential part of our beings, uniquely created by our Maker, will not die. The physical body will **go the way of all the earth** but not our spiritual body.

Therefore, there is no reason for us to fear death. We are not ending – just transitioning to another life. It is life after life.

It is much harder to deal with the death of a loved one; family or friend; someone full of years or a newborn. Have things changed? Yes and no. Things change because it is hard to say goodbye for even a little while. It makes no difference if our loved one was healthy or infirm. Saying goodbye is still difficult. There is an expression in Hebrew. It is l'hit raot, which literally means I will see (with my eyes) you again.

Torment is a favorite ploy of the enemy. There is natural grief that passes after a time of mourning but there is false or unnatural grief that continues in full intensity sometimes years after the death of a loved one. This tremendous sense of inconsolable loss often lingers.

If your level of grieving is as intense many months or years after the passing of a cherished one then perhaps you are a victim of the spirit of torment.

Torment is a spirit masquerading as natural grief. Overwhelming sadness engulfs a person. Memories haunt us of long past arguments. Painful moments are re-experienced. Mental images of your loved one encountering the passing of this life into the next are constantly before your eyes. (Remember, we do not look our best when we are born and similarly do not look our best when we transition into the world to come.)

Satan's favorite opponent is someone who is weakened and unable to defend him/herself. Through the prayer of others the person is protected.

You may pray the following prayer for yourself or someone who has experienced a recent loss.

Dear Father,

You are the giver of all life. Now is the appointed time which You chose before _____ (enter name of loved one) was born to take him/her to Yourself.

I release _____ (enter name of loved one) to You.

I forgive _____ (enter name of loved one) for all the hurtful things she/he has done to me knowingly or unknowingly. I will not dwell on the past and I ask You to cleanse me from all unpleasant memories. I do not desire to hold on to ill feelings and past mistakes.

I forgive myself for things I have said, done or thought against _____ (enter name of loved one). I know You also forgive me and I accept Your forgiveness.

In the name of Yeshua (Jesus), the name that is above every name, the name at which demons tremble, I command all spirits of torment, unforgiveness and physical pain where these memories reside in various parts of my body to leave.

I thank You for Your peace that passes all understanding and I claim Your promise that You give perfect sleep to Your beloved.

No terror by night will torment me in Yeshua's name.

Amen.

Sometimes people find it helpful to repeat this prayer daily for a period of time.

Transitions In Life

2 Kings 2:11 *¹¹Then it happened, as they continued on and talked, that suddenly a chariot of fire appeared with horses of fire, and separated the two of them; and Elijah went up by a whirlwind into heaven.*

God was transitioning Elijah, the greatest prophet in Israel from earth to Heaven. He chose a fiery chariot and team of horses as Elijah's vehicle. He fueled their journey by a whirlwind. From across the river, Elisha and the school of prophets witnessed a spectacular sight not easily forgotten.

Our lives are filled with transitions, times when we cross from one realm to the next. Being born, reaching puberty, reaching adulthood, getting married, having children and leaving this world are just a few of the transitions we may experience. These are times when our lives change drastically.

Elijah's life is an example for us of a Godly man who never wavered in his service to the Lord. Elijah's transition was as dramatic and supernatural as the way he lived his life. God used fire as Elijah's extraordinary vehicle. God also used fire to receive offerings and sacrifices from the people of Israel. It is as if Elijah's life was an offering to the Lord, which God found pleasing and acceptable.

The whirlwind is representative of great power. The chariot and horses of fire would have been sufficient but God chose to send the whirlwind as well. When God underscores something, He often will repeat it more than once or make it very dramatic. This is an example God is using to teach Elisha, the school of prophets and us. There can be no doubt of God's favor on Elijah's life.

Think of your transitions.

- ❖ Are they times when you stumble about hoping to find the correct path?
- ❖ Can you remember your transitional times or are they merely a blur?
- ❖ Are you facing some transitions in the near future life?
- ❖ Can you think of any ways to make your transitions smoother?

Praying is always a wonderful way to provide a smooth transition as we embark onto new phase of our lives.

Dear Father,

You know the new phase I am about to enter. I confess I have doubt, fear and worry. I know the past but I am unsure of the future. I ask You to wipe away all my negative thoughts and emotions.

These hindering spirits will not torment me any longer.

I believe You have a perfect plan for my life. I receive all that You desire to give me. I bind every demon in Heaven and earth trying to afflict me. Whatever I bind on earth is bound in Heaven.

I loose Your perfect peace that passes all understanding into every part of my being and into those who are close to me and are involved in this transition. I receive Your peace and will walk in it daily.

Thank You Lord for being merciful caring about my life to the smallest detail. I look forward to the new phase in my life and I welcome the smooth transition.

In the precious name of Your Son Yeshua (Jesus), I pray, Amen

Epilogue

Dear Readers,

I trust you are well established in your journey on the Highway of Holiness. It has been a joy for me to share the insights given by the Lord.

I hope this book has ministered to you and will allow you to minister to others.

May God's face always shine upon you,

Margaret

Additional Resources Available From Moriah Ministries
(http://www.moriahministries.org)

Dothan PUBLISHING

The Fifth Cup Haggadah
By Thomas D. Keck

Acquire a greater understanding and appreciation of the Last Supper. Jews and non-Jews alike can learn the significance and symbology of the Fifth Cup. Elijah's Cup, in the coming Kingdom as the prophecies of old come to fruition.   44 Pages

Davidic Dance

Learn Davidic Dances through the step-by-step instruction. Dance For Victory includes The Shout of El Shaddai and Take Me In. Worship Him In Dance includes Psalm 30, Mirad Cuan Bueno (also known as Hinei Ma Tov), It Is Good, Days Of

Elijah, El Grito Del El Shaddai (The Shout of El Shaddai) and Jew and Gentile. Dance To Be Free includes two popular worship dances easily applied to many songs.   VHS HiFi 60 min.

Mail to Moriah Ministries, PO Box 23823, Chagrin Falls OH 44023 or phone (440) 543-9304 with credit card order. Please enclose a check or money order made out to Moriah Ministries for the full amount including shipping.

Please provide the following contact information:

Name
Street Address
Address (cont.)
City
State/Province
Zip/Postal Code
E-Mail

QTY	DESCRIPTION	PRICE	S&H	TOTAL
	Dance To Be Free Video	$16	$4	
	Dance For Victory	$16	$4	
	Worship Him In Dance	$18	$4	
	Walking On The Highway Of Holiness	$9.95	$3	
	The Fifth Cup Haggadah	$4.95	$1.50	